Come Down,
O Love Divine

Sr. Maria Natella, O.P.

New Life Publishing

First edition published in 2005 by
New Life Publishing, 15 Barking Close
Luton, Beds. LU4 9HG
orders@goodnewsbooks.net

British Library Cataloguing in Publication Data
A catalogue record for this book is
available from the British Library

Bible references taken from the
Jerusalem version of the Bible.
Publishers Darton, Longman & Todd

ISBN 1 903623 21 9

Typesetting by New Life Publishing.
Printed in the UK by Print Solutions,
Wallington, Surrey.

DEDICATION

This book is dedicated to
my mum, Jean Natella,
who has been a continual
inspiration, support and strength to
my brothers Gary and Adrian and
myself throughout our lives.
Thank you for always being there
for us no matter how hard things got.

ACKNOWLEDGEMENT

I would like to thank Sr. Margarita for the inspiration she has been to me over the years, of which this book is a fruit.

Also, I would like to thank Marie Kemp, Phyl Noscoe, and Fr. Grant Maddock for their invaluable support and encouragement, and Sr. Rosaleen Shaw and Sr. Julie Marsh-Collis of my community, who worked so hard on the proof reading.

Thanks also to Gerard and Toni Pomfret, my publishers, for their continued support, enthusiasm, and encouragement throughout the writing and production of this book.

CONTENTS

Contents continued..............

.......Contents continued

Come down, O love divine,
seek thou this soul of mine,
and visit it with thine own ardour glowing;
O comforter, draw near,
within my heart appear,
and kindle it, thy holy flame bestowing.

O let it freely burn,
till earthly passions turn
to dust and ashes in its heat consuming;
and let thy glorious light
shine ever on my sight, and clothe me round,
the while my path illuming.

Let holy charity
mine outward vesture be,
and lowliness become mine inner clothing;
true lowliness of heart,
which takes the humbler part,
and o'er its own shortcomings weeps with loathing.

And so the yearning strong,
with which the soul will long,
shall far outpass the power of human telling;
for none can guess its grace,
till he become the place
wherein the Holy Spirit makes his dwelling.

i

Introduction

*T*his series of four talks was given at St. Dominic's Priory, Shirley Holms, Sway, during a weekend retreat for healing. The Hymn 'Come Down, O Love Divine' was taken as the theme and the talks centered on each verse broken down line by line. Each verse was one talk.

Whilst reading and reflecting on these talks it is important to have Healing, in its broadest sense, in mind.

By Healing, I had in mind the healing of Body, Soul and Spirit, in other words the healing of the whole person. As a Dominican sister I acknowledge that the true healer is JESUS CHRIST in the power of the HOLY SPIRIT and I understand that the greatest times where healing takes place are during the Sacramental Life of the Church.

The Sacraments are the 'outward signs of inward grace', in other words the place where one can personally encounter CHRIST JESUS present in the priest who is the 'alter Christos', the 'other Christ'.[1]

Usually, the first sacrament which we receive is the sacrament of baptism wherein the effect of 'Original Sin', the sin of our first parents, is erased. Baptism is the first sacrament of the forgiveness of sins. Baptism is therefore the first sacrament of the forgiveness of sins in which the baptised person encounters the new life of 'water and the Spirit' that Jesus speaks of in His conversation with Nicodemus: *'I tell you most solemnly, unless a man is born from on high he cannot see the kingdom of God ...I tell you most solemnly, unless a man is born through water and the Spirit, he cannot enter the kingdom of God: what is born of the flesh is flesh; what is born of the spirit is spirit.'* *(John 3: 3; 5-6.)* [2]

If we sin after baptism we have, in the Catholic Church, the Sacrament of Reconciliation, otherwise known as 'Penance' or 'Confession'. Paragraph 1446 in the Catechism of the Catholic Church states: 'Christ instituted the sacrament of Penance for all sinful members of His Church: above all for those who, since Baptism, have fallen into grave sin, and have thus lost their baptismal grace and wounded ecclesial communion. (Communion with the Mystical Body of Christ - the Church) It is to them that the sacrament of penance offers a new possibility to convert and to recover the grace of justification. The Fathers of the Church present this sacrament as 'the second plank (of salvation) after the shipwreck which is the loss of grace'. (Tertullian: Page 325 Catechism of the Catholic Church)

As well as the Sacrament of Reconciliation we also receive Healing through the Eucharist. The sacrament which is the 'source and summit' of our lives. In the Holy Eucharist we not only see the person of Christ in the sacramental species but we are encouraged to 'take and eat' for Jesus at the Last Supper said: *"This is my body which will be given for you; do this as a memorial of me.'* (*Luke 22: 19*)

We are also invited to drink of His Blood for He also said at the Last Supper: *'Drink all of you from this, for this is my blood, the blood of the covenant, which is to be poured out for many for the forgiveness of sins.'* (*Matthew 26: 28*)

The power of the Eucharistic species is tremendous and Jesus invites each one of us to 'Take and Receive' but in order to receive this tremendous gift I have to choose to be part of the Church that He founded[3] and to whom He entrusted this tremendous gift of Himself. However, another form of Healing is available to all, through what is commonly known as 'Prayer Ministry' particularly in groups where the charisms of the Holy Spirit are prevalent, i.e. charismatic renewal groups. This is where people don't just pray for you and your intentions but they 'lay their hands' on you standing as intercessors on your behalf, praying for your particular needs and, if you wish, the needs of others who you bring to the prayer.[4] The people praying will use the gifts of the Holy Spirit[5] which are given to them for this moment, to bless you. It is important to say at this point that the people who pray in this way are not praying, or should not be praying, of themselves but that they are the vessels of grace whereby the Holy Spirit flows to the person being prayed with.

It is important to state that those who are 'ministering' are not doing so out of 'self-gratification' but in a state of total abandonment to the will of God. It is also important to say that those ministering may not be in a state of grace.[6] This will not effect how efficacious the prayer is because it is GOD who heals and not those praying.

I could continue talking about the sacramental life and Prayer Ministry but that would be another series of talks. However, if you have any questions, the sisters at St. Dominic's would be only too happy for you to contact them. They will help you if they can or they will put you in touch with someone who is more qualified in the area

that you are asking about. Our Address is:
St. Dominic's Priory, Shirley Holms Road,
Lymington, Hants, SO41 8NH

Notes to Introduction :
1. *Paragraph 1548, page 346 Catechism of the Catholic church. Pub. Geoffrey Chapman: 'In the ecclesial service of the ordained minister, it is Christ Himself who is present to his church as Head of his Body, Shepherd of his flock, high priest of the redemptive sacrifice, Teacher of Truth. This is what the Church means by saying that the priest, by virtue of the sacrament of Holy Orders, acts in persona Christi Capitas: It is the same priest, Christ Jesus, whose sacred person his minister truly represents. Now the minister, by reason of the sacerdotal consecration which he has received, is truly made like to the high priest and possesses the authority to act in the power and place of the person of Christ himself (Virtue ac persona ipsius Christi).*
2. *Many Churches do not understand the need for infant baptism. To get an understanding of why an infant needs to be baptised and brought into new life with Christ, I suggest the reading of 'The Confessions of St. Augustine' by St. Augustine.*
3. *'So I now say to you: You are Peter and on this rock I will build my Church.' Matthew 16:18*
4. *This follows the prayer of the Centurion who asked for his servant to be cured without Jesus having to go to his home, see Matt. 8: 5-13.*
5. *The gifts of Prophecy, Words of Knowledge, Speaking in Tongues, the use of Sacred Scripture or pictures to clarify a point.*
6. *One can prepare to minister to another through the 'laying on of hands' by first going to the Sacrament of Reconciliation, Personal Prayer and Fasting but God can use who He wants and the defects of the 'Prayer' will not be an obstacle to God, because at the time of Praying, God is interested in the one being prayed for and not the one doing the praying.*

Verse One

Come down, O love divine,
seek thou this soul of mine,
and visit it with thine own ardour glowing;
O comforter, draw near,
within my heart appear,
and kindle it, thy holy flame bestowing.

We are told by the editors of Hymns Old and New that this wonderful hymn is attributed to Bianco da Siena (d.1434). Interestingly, our own Dominican Saint, St. Catherine, also came from Siena. The editors do say, however, that tradition has it that one R.F. Littledale was the original composer. For us though, in one sense, it is not important to know who the composer was but that we meditate on the words that have been written and handed down to us.

This hymn, as I hope you will agree, is not just a hymn but it is a prayer raising up our minds and our hearts to God. This is a prayer written from the depths of the composer's heart. It is a prayer of petition in which the composer requests that God visit their soul at one and the same time to comfort it and to rekindle the glow of faith by the fire of God's love coming to ignite it once again.

As I have already said in the introduction, I propose to meditate on this hymn verse by verse, line by line, in the light of the Healing Power of God.

Come Down, O Love Divine

What an invitation! What a cry from the heart! The second verse of the Bible reads: *'Now the earth was a formless void, there was darkness over the deep, and God's spirit hovered over the water.'* (*Genesis 1: 2*)

In the beginning there was nothing. A formless void that was nothing and in which was nothing. All was dark. There was nothing, **but** the Holy Spirit hovered. The same Holy Spirit of which the prophet Joel was to prophesy those famous words which we understand as a fore-shadowing of the great event of the Holy Spirit being poured out on the Church at Pentecost.

The prophet Joel wrote: *'After this I will pour out my spirit on all mankind.'* *(Joel 3: 1)*

In the Gospel of St. Luke we read the words of the Angel Gabriel to Mary after she has just asked how will it be possible for her, a virgin, to conceive and bear the Son of God the Most High. The Angel Gabriel said to her in answer: *'The Holy Spirit will come upon you and the power of the Most High will cover you with its shadow.'* *(Luke 1: 35)*

This is the same Holy Spirit which St. Paul experienced so powerfully in his life, an experience which led him to pray for the people of Ephesus, we read: *'Out of His infinite glory may he give you the power through His Spirit for your hidden self to grow strong.'* *(Ephesians 3: 16)*

The same Holy Spirit of which St. Paul knew that when present the Holy Spirit made it possible for life itself to possess us, for his prayer continues: *'So that Christ may live in your hearts through faith, then planted in love and built on love you will with all the saints have the strength to grasp the breadth and the length, the height and the depth, until knowing the love of Christ, which is beyond all knowledge, you are filled with the utter fulness of God.'* *(Ephesians 3: 16-19)*

The Holy Spirit, the giver of life, hovered over nothing. Mary, the Virgin Mother of God, would later proclaim, 'Nothing is impossible to God.' For where there was nothing in her virginal womb God, through the hovering of the Holy Spirit, brought life into that which held nothing.

Thus, the nothing of the void was impossible for God, for God, the Author of Life, confers life and so into the nothing came life when God said: *'Let there be light.'* (*Genesis 1: 3*)

The Holy Spirit conferred on the formless void - **form.** What was once **not, now was.** The power of the infinity of God creates matter and all living things from - **nothing.** The power of the **infinite** God hovered - to confer life, to make the unknown - knowable, the unseen - seen, the invisible - visible. The power of the **infinity** of God is the power of **life,** the power of **love.** The power of the **infinity** of God both forms and informs.

As we join in the composer's prayer we ask ourselves How informed are we? Meaning by that not how much knowledge our minds contain but how much our very souls have been formed from within by the power of the Most High God hovering over us, waiting for us to say: 'Let what You have said be done to me. Let there be light – in my heart, mind and soul. Let my darkness be turned into day.'

When Mary, the Mother of our Lord and *our* Mother, said:

'*Let what you have said be done to me,*' *(Luke 1:38)*, she was allowing the words of the prophet Ezekiel to be fulfilled. For he had once prophesied: '*I mean to display the Holiness of my Great Name, which has been profaned among the nations, which you have profaned among them. And the nations will learn that I am YAHWEH* - it is the LORD who speaks - when I display My Holiness [7] for your sake before their eyes. Then I am going to take you from among the nations and gather you together from all the foreign countries, and bring you home to your own land. I shall pour clean water over you and you will be cleansed; I shall cleanse you of all your defilement and your idols. I shall give you a new heart, and put a new spirit in you; I shall remove the heart of stone from your bodies and give you a heart of flesh instead. I shall put My Spirit in you..., and make you keep My laws and sincerely respect My observances.*' *(Ezekiel 36: 23-28)*

*A thought on respecting GOD (Note 7)
In writing this passage I realised that whenever one reads the name YAHWEH in the Old Testament it is always written with capital letters because of the respect given to the name. This set me pondering on how much I respect the name of my LORD. I realised that I did not treat GOD, when writing about Him, with any real respect. Thus at this point in writing I have decided that from now on when I write anything pertaining to GOD, FATHER, SON and HOLY SPIRIT, I shall write with capitals. This is having the effect of challenging me to think about the respect I give to my fellow men and women, for I am called not just

to love GOD with all my heart, but also to love my neighbour and myself ....It is amazing how when one preaches one always ends up preaching to oneself before anyone else!

When we pray in earnest, 'Come Down, O Love Divine,' we are asking that we too would be cleansed of all our defilement; that we too would be cleansed of all our idols; that we would have our hearts of stone removed and have hearts of flesh instead. Indeed, we need to know something of 'Salvation History' if these words of Ezekiel are to mean anything to us in the very depth of our being.

The heart of stone that Ezekiel refers to was the heart of Israel given to them by GOD Himself: the ten commandments written on two tablets of stone. The ten commandments became for the people of Israel the heart of their lives with the Torah (the Book of the Law) developing around them. JESUS, if you recall, would later tell the people; *'I have come not to abolish the Law but to fulfill it.'* JESUS, in Himself, became the new Law – He, in Himself, with His death and resurrection, became the New Heart of Israel and for all who would accept Him, He gave eternal life.

GOD the FATHER, 'displayed the holiness of His great name' before their eyes. He gave His people a new heart and a new spirit. He did this when Mary gave her Fiat to be the Mother of the WORD incarnate ... the WORD which had: *'... existed from the beginning, that we have heard, that we have seen with our own eyes; that we have watched and touched with our own hands.'* (1 John 1: 1)

JESUS, the only begotten SON of the FATHER. JESUS, who came to fulfil the Law and not to abolish it, He in Himself is the new heart, the heart of flesh replacing the heart of stone.

In the Catechism paragraph 2563 we read: 'The heart is the dwelling-place where I AM, where I live; according to the semitic or biblical expression, the heart is the place to 'which I withdraw'. The heart is our hidden centre, beyond the grasp of our reason and of others; only the SPIRIT of GOD can fathom the human heart and know it fully. The heart is the place of decision, deeper than our psychic drives. It is the place of truth, where we choose life or death. It is the place of encounter, because as the image of GOD we live in relation: it is the place of covenant.'

How often do we find ourselves saying that we don't really know why we do the things we do? How often have we got up in the morning and been in a 'good' mood but by dinner time that mood has changed. We feel quite miserable but if anyone was to ask us what had happened to bring about this change we know that our answer would be a limp one because all we could say is 'I don't know.'

Only GOD knows who and what we really are. He knows when we are truthful and He knows when we are lying to others and to ourselves even though we don't know that that is what we are actually doing. GOD is the one who holds the 'blue-print' for us and so He is the only one we can go to if we want to plunge to the depths of ourselves.

In the past few years the trend has been to 'Get to know yourself'. This has been tried through various psychological exercises and self-awareness courses, but in the end if we are our own starting point we will never know who we are or indeed who we could become because we can only come back to our own finite self.

JESUS once asked the disciples a very important question. He asked them *'Who do you say I am?'* It was only when He asked this question that Peter was able to make the statement of faith that JESUS was 'THE CHRIST'. When we begin to ask this question of ourselves, when we begin to fathom who GOD is for us, then and only then do we begin to discover our true selves. It is only when we realise that our starting point was not when we were conceived by our parents but when we were in the mind of GOD before time came into being.

There are many 'Inner Healing' prayers that we can pray to be healed of things in our past but no matter how good the prayer is, it usually only takes us to the point of our conception. If our conception by our parents is the starting point for healing in our lives we will not go very far before we stumble and get hurt again because in fact to start at conception is to start with us being conceived into original sin. If the fall is my starting point then I will never come to understand the 'wonder of my being'. If my starting point is my being a thought in the mind of GOD, who is in Himself, infinite goodness, then my starting point on the road to healing is good news itself.

If my starting point is goodness itself, love itself, infinity itself, then my healing becomes possible if I go to the source of my life, GOD Himself. If my starting point is GOD then the Scriptures take on a new dimension, for as they depict the Salvation History of mankind so they show salvation history for each individual.

Every word of Sacred Scripture takes on a new dimension, because as I read the words of Scripture I begin to realise that I am called to echo the response that Mary, the Virgin Mother of GOD made to the angel Gabriel at the moment of the Annunciation: *'Let what you have said be done to me.'* I pray that the WORD of GOD becomes flesh for me and those I know, I then realise the power I have within my reason. Reason which is now formed and informed by the WORD of GOD Himself, through the power of the HOLY SPIRIT, that every decision I make in truth is a choice between life or death. If my starting point is not

9

GOD then I will never fully grasp what St. Paul prays for the Ephesians which is that their *'inner selves may grow strong.'*

The choice of life or death is ours but I ask how informed are our choices?

The heart 'is the place of covenant.'

In John's Gospel we read: *'FATHER, may they be one in us, as you are in me and I am in You.... ... with Me in them and You in Me, may they be so completely one that the world will realise that it was You that sent Me and that I have loved them as much as You loved Me'.* (John 17: 21,23)

Just stop and think for a moment about that last line: *'I have loved them with as much love as You loved Me'.*

GOD is infinite and He loves the SON with that infinite love. He pours His infinite love into us!

As the words of the prophet Ezekiel, the words of the Catechism and the words of St. John's Gospel begin to inform our minds and hearts we begin to understand that we are faced with a series of personal questions:
- Do I want to turn away from idols - the new car, the new wallpaper, the new clothes ... keeping up with my neighbour if not trying to 'out do' him?

10

• Do I want to be brought back from exile - the sins that I keep committing?

• Do I want to be cleansed of all defilement - am I prepared to turn off the television when it shows things that are contrary to the Gospel or cease reading magazines and books that are not in keeping with the love that Christ poured out for us on the cross?

• Do I really want to receive a new heart - do I want CHRIST Himself to come and make His home in me?

Mary, the Mother of God, the lowly handmaid, she who was conceived without sin, accepted the gift that GOD was offering her but in a way that no one else throughout time ever will. She, the young girl of fourteen or fifteen gave her fiat, her yes to GOD and conceived the only begotten SON of GOD, JESUS the CHRIST. Mary conceived the SON of GOD and proceeded to sing a hymn of praise that has been sung down through the ages:

'My soul proclaims the greatness of the LORD   *(Luke 1:46)*
My spirit exults in GOD my SAVIOUR   *(Luke 1:47)*
because He has looked on His lowly handmaid ... *(Luke 1:48)*
- Holy is His name ...   *(Luke 1:49)*
- HE has shown the power of His arm,   *(Luke 1:51)*
- HE has routed the proud of heart ...
- The hungry He has filled with good things,   *(Luke 1:53)*
- The rich sent empty away.'

Mary, at such a young age understood her 'nothingness', her 'emptiness' and it was this that enabled her to cry out to the angel: *'Let what you have said be done to me.'* *(Luke 1: 38)*

Are we, are you, truly hungry for the LORD, are we really thirsting for our GOD or when we are asked to make up our minds, do we respond in the same manner as the rich young man: *'A member of one of the leading families put this question to Him, 'Good Master, what have I to do to inherit eternal life? JESUS said to him, 'Why do you call me good? No one is good but GOD alone. You know the commandments: You must not commit adultery; You must not kill; You must not steal; You must not bring false witness; Honour your father and your mother.' He replied, 'I have kept these from my earliest days until now,' and when JESUS heard this He said, 'There is still one thing you lack. Sell all that you own and distribute the money to the poor, and you will have treasure in heaven; then come, follow me.' But when he heard this he was full of sadness because he was very rich.'* *(Luke 18: 18-23)*

GOD the FATHER wants to overshadow us with His SPIRIT that we might be filled, as St. Paul writes in his letter to the Ephesians: *'To be filled with the utter fulness of GOD'*

We come before the LORD pleading to be healed but are

12

we ready and indeed willing to give up all else to receive Him who is 'The Healer'?

Seek thou this soul of mine.

This line is a little unusual isn't it? The composer is asking GOD to seek him when JESUS invites us to seek Him: *'Seek, and you shall find. 'Knock, and the door shall be opened.'* (Matthew 7: 7-11)

Is the composer at a stage in his life where he feels that he has lost the sense of all direction? Is he 'lost' and needs to be 'found' and is there only one 'person' who can see where he is and can help him out of the state that he finds himself in: the omnipotent, all seeing, all knowing, GOD?

This line betrays a great confidence in GOD. He knows that all he has to do is ask and He will come to his aid. One senses that he knows that GOD is incarnate that He became man in order to restore all people to their former glory before the fall and indeed that He went one step further and gave all people the invitation to be His co-heirs, the first among many brothers.

'Seek thou this soul of mine.' In Holy Scripture we are conscious of the times that JESUS went out of His way to

meet people where they were most comfortable:

- Nicodemus
- The Samaritan Woman
- His own disciples
  .... to name but a few.

JESUS went to where they were:

- Nicodemus: the Night-Time Rendezvous
- The Samaritan Woman: Jacob's Well
- The Disciples: The Shore Line, the Tax Booth,
  the Sycamore Tree

JESUS will come to us wherever we are even if it is in the 'heart of a storm' as He did with His disciples to teach them that they may be asked to take a step in faith wherever they may find themselves. We read in John's Gospel: *'That evening the disciples went down to the shore of the lake and got into a boat to make for Capernaum on the other side of the lake. It was getting dark by now and JESUS still hadn't rejoined them. The wind was strong and the sea was getting rough. They had rowed three or four miles when they saw JESUS walking on the lake and coming towards the boat. This frightened them but He said; 'It is I. Do not be afraid.' They were for taking Him into the boat, but in no time it reached the shore at the place they were heading for.' (John 6: 16-21)*

14

In this passage of Scripture JESUS shows us an incredible message and that is that we do not have to make our lives 'right' or 'perfect' before we can invite JESUS to come and take possession of our hearts and souls. Indeed, if we wait until that moment we will miss the opportunity of ever knowing what it is like to have JESUS 'make His home in us.'

JESUS walks three to four miles across the stormy lake in the pitch dark in order to reach His disciples. He would have been soaked through with the spray from the water blown up by the wind let alone by the rain pouring down on Him all the time. In doing such a deed He shows us that He is Master of the elements through the power of the HOLY SPIRIT who came, and descended on Him at His own baptism in the Jordan.

JESUS is showing us that as the HOLY SPIRIT brought order out of the chaos of the formless void in Genesis, so He in the Power of the same HOLY SPIRIT can bring order into the hearts of men. What is important to note here is that the disciples are not recorded as having called out to JESUS for help. This tells us that JESUS will come to us even when we are not yet ready to receive Him and that it is only by receiving Him in the mess that order will then reign in our lives and in the lives of those around us.

JESUS brings order for his disciples and His command is

total. Incredibly before they can even talk to Him they find themselves at the very place they had originally set out for. This is also important for us to see. Often, people believe that if they were to 'let GOD into their lives' they would have to change their lives completely, that they would be asked by GOD to change the direction that they had planned out for themselves. Here, JESUS shows us that if we let Him have control of our lives He will not only 'calm the storm' but we will find ourselves at the place we were wanting to get to with no real effort on our part.

Why are we so afraid of letting everything go in order that we can fully 'grasp' Him and make Him our treasure instead?

Doesn't the Devil have a field day with us all!

The choice is for you and me to make: Life or Death? What do you choose?

Visit it with thine own ardour glowing.

Let us halt in our tracks and let GOD take control of our

lives. The thought that crosses my mind is that if we don't choose Him then every choice that we make will only lead to death because all life is found in Him alone.

If we don't let Him in then what we understand to be life is actually only mere existence because only in Him can we have life and have it to the full. He tells us: *'I came that you might have life and have it to the full.' (John's Gospel)*

We also read: *'You study scriptures, believing in them that you will have eternal life; now these same scriptures testify to Me, and yet you refuse to come to Me for life.' (John 5:39)*

JESUS came that we might have life and have it to the full. He explains that the Scriptures testify to Him and in them there is life but that life doesn't stop there. He Himself is the source of all life: *'In the beginning was the WORD: the WORD was with GOD and the WORD was GOD. He was with GOD in the beginning. Through Him all things came to be, not one thing had its being but through Him.' (John 1: 1-3)*

JESUS, the CHRIST, the incarnate WORD of GOD did not only become flesh of our flesh in order to die for us so that we might be freed from the lasting effects of man's fall from grace when Adam committed the Original Sin. He went further and gave us Himself as **food** and **drink**. He actually made it possible through the Eucharistic

Species to literally come into our very being and effect us from within, literally in-forming us, changing us into *Himself* and in so doing give us the gift of Eternal Life. We read in Chapter 6 of St. John's Gospel: *'I tell you most solemnly, if you do not eat the **flesh** of the SON of MAN and drink His **blood** you will not have life in you. Anyone who does eat **My flesh** and drink **My blood** has eternal life and I shall raise him up on the last day.'* (John 6: 53, 54)

In St. John's account of the 'Cleansing of the Temple' he takes up one of the psalms and uses it to describe the actions of *Jesus: 'Zeal for My FATHER'S house will devour Me.'* (John 2: 17, Ps 69: 9)

We often only apply this to the Temple in Jerusalem and to JESUS speaking about His own body, the nature of man that He possessed. I would like to take this one step further and remind ourselves that it is also said of the newly baptised that they too are 'Temples of the HOLY SPIRIT.' So we can rightly say that JESUS' zeal for us will in the end quite literally 'devour Him'.

Towards the end of St. John's crucifixion account we hear JESUS crying out towards the end of His struggle: *'I am thirsty.'* (John 19: 28)

St. Augustine, one of the early Father's of the Church wrote: 'Whether we realise it or not, prayer is the encounter of GOD'S thirst with ours. GOD thirsts that we might thirst for Him.' (Catechism 2560)

JESUS thirsts for our souls to the point of literally being devoured by His great zeal for us when He died on the cross for us.

When we speak of GOD'S thirst for us we cannot but help recall JESUS' words to the Samaritan Woman that He met by Jacob's well: *'Jesus replied: 'If only you knew what GOD is offering and who it is that is saying to you: Give me a drink, you would have been the one to ask, And He would have given you living water... ...Whoever drinks this water will get thirsty again; but anyone who drinks the water that I shall give will never get thirsty again: the water that I shall give will turn into a spring inside him, welling up to eternal life.' (John 4:10; 13,14)*

JESUS thirsts for us that we might thirst for Him unto the point of death for reading further in St. John's crucifixion account we find: *'When they came to JESUS, they found He was already dead, so instead of breaking His legs one of the soldiers pierced His side with a lance; and immediately there came out blood and water.'*

If we look at the Prophet Ezekiel chapter 47:1-12, we have the prophesy of the water coming from the right side of the Temple, this is fulfilled when the water comes from the right side of CHRIST as He hung on the cross. Remember that He had referred to Himself as the Temple when He said: *'Destroy this temple and in three days I will raise it up.'*

What is important to realise is that the water that Ezekiel spoke of, which brought healing for anything that lived in it prefigures the water that flowed from the side of CHRIST and that that in turn is the water of Baptism. (The leaves on the trees on either side of the bank of the water also bring healing.)

It is so clear that GOD thirsts for us body, soul and spirit. The question we need to ask of ourselves and answer with honesty is: How thirsty are we for the things of GOD and indeed for GOD Himself? Can we sing out with the psalmist:
'O GOD, you are my GOD, for you I long;
For you my soul is thirsting.
My body pines for you
Like a dry, weary land without water.'

GOD has such a thirst, a zeal for us that He was prepared to become **incarnate** that we would know just how much He does love us. To see the heart of GOD is to look at JESUS on the cross with His side split open, for there is the heart of GOD exposed and vulnerable for us to do with Him what we will. Let us not fail Him with a mediocre response, or no response at all. Let us 'run and not grow weary' as the song would tell us. Let us never stop seeking GOD with all our heart, all our strength and all our soul. GOD gives us everything. He gave us the world He created and His own **body** broken for us to eat and His **blood poured** out for us to drink. Let us run to Him and allow ourselves to be consumed by His passion that we might become passionate for GOD, giving over our lives to Him 'unto death' as the 'Finally Professed Religious' vows to do.

Let us conclude this section with the beautiful words from the Song of Songs:
'Set me like a seal on your heart,
like a seal on your arm.
For love is strong as Death,
Jealousy relentless as Sheol.
The flash of it is a flash of fire,
A flame of YAHWEH Himself.
Love no flood can quench,
No torrents drown.' *(Song of Songs 8: 6-7)*

Let us let nothing come between us and our love for GOD, because only if we allow Him to love us and we then learn to love Him in response will we really be able to love others with a genuine love. Any love that has its source in ourselves can only be broken and fragmented because of the effect of Original Sin, only through the love of GOD will our love become more and more a perfected love. Let us then strive to love GOD, our neighbours and ourselves with a perfect love.

O comforter, draw near.

The composer prays to be consumed with the fire of burning love. A 'fire' that will not only 'set him alight' but that knowing JESUS CHRIST has come and made His home in him, he prays that he will experience a comfort deep within his being: a *'peace that the world cannot give'*.

St. John in his gospel writes: *'Peace I bequeath you, My own peace I give you, a peace that the world cannot give, this is my gift to you. Do not let your hearts be troubled or afraid.'* (*John 14: 27*)

Just think about this gift of peace that JESUS died to bring us, you and me, for a moment. Think back over your life and see if you have ever felt this peace. A deep peace that came upon you when all around you seemed to be chaos. A time of peace amongst a time when nothing in life seemed to be making any sense. A peace that was a gift to you that you yourself could not induce no matter how many candles you lit, tapes you played, chocolates you ate or clothes that you bought. A peace that came from within you and with the sense of peace there was the

22

understanding that no matter how bad things got all would be well in the end. A peace that enabled you to carry on amidst the darkness and gloom, the uncertainty that had encompassed you.

Earlier in Chapter 14 we read: *'If you ask for anything in My name I will do it. If you love Me you will keep My commandments. I shall ask the FATHER, And He will give you another **advocate** to be with you forever. The SPIRIT of TRUTH whom the world can never receive since it neither sees nor knows Him; but you know Him, because He is with you, He is in you. I will not leave you orphans; I will come back to you. In a short time the world will no longer see Me; but you will see Me, because I live and you will live. On that day you will understand that I am in My FATHER, and you in Me and I in you. Anybody who receives My commandments and keeps them will be one who loves Me; and anyone who loves Me will be loved by My FATHER, and I shall love him and show Myself to him.'* (*John 14:14f*)

Stop for a moment and read these words over and over again because they contain such a tremendously powerful message of the love of GOD for us His creation.

The GOD who made the universe and all things in it, who created you and me, actually makes His home in us. The Israelites had the privilege of GOD meeting with Moses and Aaron at the Tent of Meeting. Solomon built an incredible Temple so that God need not 'dwell' in a tent anymore. His father, King David, had conceived the idea of a house for GOD whilst he was looking at his own palace one day. He saw that as he, an earthly king lived in such a tremendous palace, made of gold and all the other precious metals and fine woods that there could be gathered. King David then decided that GOD should 'dwell' in a house that far surpassed his own, only GOD told him that he was not to build it himself but that his own son Solomon was to be the builder. That palace was built but GOD chose to come closer to His creation and became flesh of our flesh, being born of the Virgin Mary. But, this GOD who loves us so much didn't stop even there, He condescended to come and make His home in us, in a real way in the Eucharistic Species.

I pause for a moment to recall the words of a small book that I was given, which was written in 1881 and was then in the ninth edition. The book was written by Fr. F. Lewis de Granada, O.P. It is a treasure because it contains so many rich things on each page that leaves one pondering long after the book has been finished and put away. The title of the book is 'A memorial of a Christian Life'. I would like to quote two passages from it that will emphasise the point I am making about the greatness of our GOD who chose not only to die for us but who chose to live in us.

Page 289-290: 'Had thy goodness condescended to come unto me in any other manner, it still had been an effect of thy great mercy; but now, O Lord, thou hast not only been pleased to visit me, but has also vouchsafed to enter under my roof, to dwell in me, to transform me into thee, and make me one and the same thing with thyself, by so admirable a union, that thy sacred mouth has found nothing more fit to express it, than to compare it with the union thou hast with thy Almighty Father: this is what far surpasses, and is altogether incomprehensible to human understanding. David wondered at thy care of man, when he said, *'What is man that thou art mindful of him?'* *(Psalm 8:5).* But it is far more to be admired, that God not only remembers man but that he makes himself man for him, that he dwells with him, that he dies for him, that he feeds him with his own flesh and blood, and makes himself one and the same thing with him. Solomon begged of God, if it were possible, that he would actually reside in the temple he had been so many years in building; but it is a much greater wonder that God, who dwells in the heavens, should, after a far more excellent manner, make his abode in a poor soul, who has scarcely laboured so much as one day only to prepare him a lodging. All created nature is rapt with admiration to see God made man, to see him descend from heaven to earth, and continue nine months enclosed in a virgin's womb. These indeed are wonderful things, and fit to be admired; but it is also true, that the womb of this virgin was filled with the Holy Ghost, and it was purer than the stars of heaven, and so a lodging made worthy of the Son of God. But that this Lord should dwell in my heart, that he would choose for a habitation a place so filthy and full of darkness, is the highest and most amazing excess to which his mercy could descend.'

Read these words. Pray through these words. Don't just race through them because they hold for ourselves a treasure so rich in the gift that GOD wants us to understand in order that we might be able to co-operate with the graces that He out of His infinite goodness has seen fit to bestow on us. To help you understand and grasp this even more I quote once more from the same source: Page 233-234: 'During these three days (Fr. de Granada encouraged his readers to take three days to prepare for receiving Christ in the Eucharist) pray to the Most Holy Trinity; address yourself everyday to one of the three persons separately, to the end they may give you the grace and purity which is necessary for this holy communion. Have recourse particularly to the Blessed Virgin, beseeching her by that fervour and that admirable devotion with which she conceived in her womb the Son of God, and received him in her arms after he was born, to obtain for you the grace to receive him in your soul. Beg of her, by that tenderness and those transports with which she herself communicated, and received the sacred body of her Son, after his ascent into heaven, to obtain for you some part in the grace and love which he made her feel when he gave himself to her. In this prayer to the Queen of Heaven, make particular reflections on the lively faith, the devotion, the tears, and the joy with which she received her Son in the sacramental species, in expectation of the time when she would see him in her glory. For if you can conceive anything of the faith and love of this holy creature, that is, with how much firmness and certainty she believed that in this consecrated bread there was truly her Son's precious body, what affection she had for him, and what desire to see him, possess him, and embrace him in her heart; you will, without doubt, comprehend something of the sentiments of that divine soul, and of the heavenly content she found in herself at the time of her communion. Beg of her some of her devotion, and she will transmit to you some spark of that divine fire, the least of which would be sufficient to prepare you as you ought for this wonderful feast.'

Having pondered the words of Fr. de Granada O.P. that were written so long ago and yet hold much meaning for us today, can we see that we have in some way lost the sense of the divine? Can we admit that we have lost the understanding of what is happening to us when the FATHER, SON and HOLY SPIRIT make their home in us? If we think of how Mary, the Virgin Mother of Our LORD felt when she was carrying Him in her womb we too will get the sense of what it means to have GOD make His home in us. If we reflect on the joy Mary felt as her Son kicked in her womb we will begin to recognise when CHRIST is 'moving ' in us. We will more readily identify with St. Paul when he states that 'It is no longer I that live, but CHRIST who lives in me'. As we ponder the divine in us we will begin to change the way we speak, the way we think and the way we act because we will know what a high calling we have. We will understand what it means when we read in Sacred Scripture that we have been made in the image and likeness of GOD. St. Ambrose, one of the early Church Fathers wrote: 'If you believe you will conceive and generate the Word of God.'

We will be GOD orientated instead of being self-minded, self-willed, selfish. A longing will be born in us of loving GOD and all that He has made including those who irritate us, criticise us, put us down, we will be able to love because we will know that we have been loved by GOD so much.

We will not only experience a joy that the world cannot give, a peace that the world cannot give, but we will live a life that the world did not give us. **We** will become **fully alive** instead of just existing from day to day, from one moment to the next, from one episode of our favourite television programme to the next. **No!** We will have life and have it to the full, and we will also have the graces we need to live our lives to the full.

St. John also wrote: *'As the FATHER has loved Me, so I have loved you.... I have told you this so that My own joy may be in you and your joy be complete .... I shall not call you servants anymore ... I shall call you friends, ...You did not choose Me, no I chose you; ...'* (John 15: 16)

GOD made us and loved us. In loving us He gave His life for us. In giving His **life** for us he made us co-heirs with Him. In making us co-heirs with Him He has made us become as He is. St. Augustine, another Father of the Church once wrote: 'God became man, that man might become GOD.'

Ponder these words and be still, know that He is God and He loves you unto His own death that we might share in His life, in heaven for all eternity.

JESUS died for us, He comforts us, He shares His joy with us, His peace with us, His life with us but, and this is important to realise, this does not mean that we will be freed from sorrow. Indeed, it shall be quite the contrary because to follow Him is to embrace His cross, **completely**. Precisely because He sends us His **comforter,** the HOLY SPIRIT we will have all that we need to help us embrace that cross, the cross that He invites us to pick up every day and follow Him.

> NO cross = NO death
> NO death = NO resurrection
> NO resurrection = NO glory
> NO glory = NO eternity

If we don't embrace the cross then we will never know the deep joy of being a true disciple. St. John clearly warns us who would follow Him to the cross: *'If the world hates you, remember that it hated Me before you. If you belonged to the world the world would love you as its own; but because you do not belong to the world, because My choice withdrew you from the world therefore the world hates you.'* (John 15: 18-19)

If you drag the cross you will only find it getting heavier because you will gather with it a lot of rubbish. If you embrace the cross, then you only carry the cross and we know that the LORD would never give us anything that was too hard for us to bear. If we are unsure we only need to remind ourselves of when Simon of Cyrene was challenged to help the LORD carry His cross. Simon only had to carry it a short distance, JESUS carried it most of the way and if we need to be encouraged further it is only JESUS who was asked by the FATHER to die on the cross.

Within my heart appear

JESUS' choice of us withdraws us from the world and because He has singled us out the world does turn against us. Thus the composer doesn't stop at only requesting that he 'feel' the comfort of GOD but he goes further and asks that He comes and makes His home in his heart in a visible and tangible way.

The way Sacred Scripture guides us in letting our LORD and SAVIOUR come into our lives is through Sacred Scripture itself and through the Eucharistic Species. (Some of this I have already mentioned especially when quoting from Fr. de Granada's book, pages 233-234.)

St. Luke clearly spells out in his gospel how everyone can be truly happy in JESUS: *'Now as he was speaking, a woman in the crowd raised her voice and said, 'Happy the womb that bore you and the breasts that you sucked!' But HE replied, 'Still happier are those who hear the WORD of GOD and keep it.' (Luke 11: 27)*

The message from St. Luke could not be any clearer. We are to not only read or listen to the words of Sacred Scripture and then immediately forget them. **No,** we are encouraged to hear the WORD of GOD and keep it. This means that we are invited or challenged to read or listen to the WORD of GOD and chew it over and over again in our minds and hearts until one day the WORD itself becomes flesh in us. One of the Dominican mottos encourages us to 'Become what you pray.' Indeed, we do become what we read or what we gaze upon, be it for good or ill. The challenge thrown out to us is that we need to be very careful about the material we digest, conversation, reading or viewing, if we want to bear good fruit, that is. If we are not worried about who and what we are becoming then we will not think twice about the type of magazines we read, or the daily paper we glance at before going to work. We will not think twice about the sort of company we keep or the conversation matter that we share in. We will not think twice about the kind of videos we watch, the films or television that we see.

If we do care about who and what we are, if we do think about our final end then we will examine everything and make sure that nothing that is contrary to the Gospel of CHRIST will be seen or participated in.

But the question is, 'Do you care?' Are you making decisions about what forms you or are you allowing the world to form you into its image and likeness: well, after all it is the easier road to take and there are many avenues and adventures to be had along the path of life! St. Matthew in his gospel writes a few words of warning which are most apt to be mentioned at this point: *'Enter by the narrow gate, since the road that leads to perdition is wide and spacious, and many take it; but it is a narrow gate and a hard road that leads to life, and only a few find it.'* (Matthew 7: 13-14)

The width of the road is as narrow as the cross that we carry, it is as narrow as ourselves because when all is said and done we are personally responsible for the choices we make. Many people will say 'But, I am only human.' At this point if we reflect on those words carefully we condemn ourselves as we say them because although the old saying ' to err is human' confirms these words, these words are actually an insult to GOD in one way. Ponder for a moment that truth that JESUS, the CHRIST, took on our human nature and it was within that humanity that He saved us from death. As St. Paul tells us in his letter to the Philippians: *'Although His state was divine, he did not cling to His equality with GOD, but He emptied Himself to assume the condition of a slave[8], and became as all men are; and being as all men are He was humbler yet, even to accepting death, death on a cross.'*

JESUS, therefore, was fully human and fully divine and in being fully human He throws out to us the challenge to not give in to temptation. HE challenges us to grow in our humanity, grow in the dignity that GOD Himself conferred on all mankind when He created us. The Catholic Catechism will tell us that all men are affected by concupiscence (the inclination to sin that is left in our nature after the fall) but, just because we have the inclination to sin it does not equate that we have to sin. I, and I alone choose whether I am going to give in to temptation and sin or, in the power of the HOLY SPIRIT, I am going to fight the temptation. It is not easy and that is why it is the *narrow* road, because only a few really manage it. The question for us to ask of ourselves is do we want to be one of the few or do we want to be one of the many?

St. Matthew in his gospel describes what it means to be a true disciple: *'It is not those who say to Me, 'LORD, LORD', who will enter the kingdom of heaven, but the person who does the will of My FATHER in heaven. When the day comes many will say to Me, 'LORD, LORD, did we not prophesy in your name, cast out demons in your name, work miracles in your name?' Then I shall tell them to their faces: 'I have never known you; away from me you evil men!' Therefore, everyone who listens to these words of mine and acts on them will be like a sensible man who built his house on rock.'* (Matthew 7: 21-24)

Let us heed His warning, let us not just talk about the things of GOD but let us live in the way GOD intended us to live - in communion with Himself now and for all eternity.

St. John also encourages us to listen to the WORD of GOD and act upon what we hear: *'A child of GOD listens to the words of GOD; if you refuse to listen, it is because you are not GOD'S children.'* (John 8:47)

What could be plainer? If we are feeling that in some way all of this is too hard for us to do let us be encouraged by the fact that Mary, the Mother of GOD, was herself asked also to listen before anything else happened. The root word of **'listen'** comes from the word which means 'to obey'. Things now begin to become clear: we understand that it is through Mary's listening (obedience) that she overturned the disobedience of Eve. Through Mary's listening she was able to hear and then respond to what GOD was asking of her; to conceive the WORD and bring Him forth into a hungry, waiting world. When Eve disobeyed, Adam chose to do as she suggested and in obeying Eve and the serpent Adam, the first man, brought disobedience into our nature. When we choose to **listen** to GOD we ourselves are actually choosing to play our part in the Salvific History, the turning of Man's minds and hearts back to GOD.

'Mary, do not be afraid, you have won GOD'S favour. **Listen!** *You are to conceive and bear a son and you must name Him JESUS.' (Luke 1: 31)*

Mary did listen and because she listened and chose to accept what was being asked of her. (Remember that she was only 14 or 15 years of age at this time.) Mary allowed the WORD of GOD to become flesh of our flesh. She listened and she obeyed. She was her son's first disciple, **before** He had even been conceived in her!

St. John once again encourages us: *'If you make My WORD your home you will indeed be my disciples, and you will learn the truth and the truth will set you free.' (John 8:31-32)*

So, our happiness lies in the WORD of GOD and our ability to **listen** and promptly respond to that WORD with our own 'Fiat', our own 'Yes'. To allow the WORD to cut through us, but to cut 'more finely than any double-edged sword'.

The invitation is clear, will we respond with a firm 'Yes' or a firm 'No'? It is important to realise that in this choice there is no middle ground: either we want to follow in the footsteps of CHRIST or we don't. Moses said to the Israelites: *'I put before you life or death ...'* JESUS speaks to us using the same words: *'I put before you life or death.'* When He calls us to make a choice one way or the other remember that we are not invited to choose one ideology over another, one school of religious thought or another, one faith over another. If we choose life then we choose Him, for He tells us so clearly; *'I Am the WAY, the TRUTH and the LIFE.'*

What do you choose?

And kindle it, thy holy flame bestowing

The invitation at the end of the preceding section was for us to 'Hear the WORD of GOD and keep it'. The composer doesn't stop there because he knows that JESUS Himself was enabled in His humanity to remain faithful to the FATHER'S will by allowing the HOLY SPIRIT to both guide Him and to work through Him. Through the power of the HOLY SPIRIT the WORD of GOD, becomes a very active force in our lives. Because we allow Him to be active **in us** He is able to be present to the world that thirsts for Him even if it is not conscious of doing so.

When we begin to turn our hearts and minds to GOD we become very conscious of what life would be without Him. Indeed, the closer one gets to Him in the spiritual journey we discover that we are conscious that the sin, that before we would not have spoken of as a sin, begins to be a greater gulf that we build between Him and ourselves. We find no consolation in people telling us that 'that is such a small thing I would not worry about it, GOD is bigger than that'. For us, because of the activity of the HOLY SPIRIT in us we know that we have sinned even if the other can not see it as such.

Despite what others might tell us we long to run to the Sacrament of Penance and ask forgiveness of our sin and to hear the priest proclaim in CHRIST, 'I absolve you of all your sins'. Then, and only then, does peace once more flood into our previously troubled soul. We have a taste of what the disciples felt when JESUS appeared to them after the resurrection: *'In the evening of that same day, the first day of the week, the doors were closed in the room where the disciples were, for fear of the Jews. JESUS came and stood among them. He said to them, '**Peace** be with you', and showed them His hands and His side. The disciples were filled with joy when they saw the LORD and He said to them again 'Peace be with you. 'As the FATHER sent Me so I am sending you. After saying this He breathed on them and said: 'Receive the HOLY SPIRIT ...' (John 19: 19-21)*

We are very much aware of what happened when they received the HOLY SPIRIT. They were filled with a joy so glorious that they wanted to 'go out to the whole world and proclaim the Good News.' Nothing like this had ever happened to them before. Take note, that it is when JESUS shows them the wounds in His hands and His side that they are filled with joy. Then, having been filled with a joy that was beyond their imaginings, they were open then to receive an even greater gift, the gift of the **comforter** Himself, the HOLY SPIRIT. The disciples knew in a moment that JESUS was never going to leave them because the HOLY SPIRIT, the breath of GOD would always be there to guide and comfort them. They knew that He really was never going to 'leave them orphans'.

We too can begin to experience this peace and joy, this incredible comfort, when we open ourselves to being filled with the HOLY SPIRIT. We need to put ourselves in the same position as the disciples were when they received the Holy Spirit. We need to read the passage of John's Gospel over and over again. They did not receive the HOLY SPIRIT when they were praying together, they were praying but it wasn't that which opened the way for them to receive the HOLY SPIRIT. The door was opened when JESUS quite simply showed them the wounds in His hands and His side, for we are told in scripture that it is 'by His wounds that we are healed.'

Before He showed them His wounds He said to them 'Peace be with you.' When they had received this peace, a peace that only JESUS can bestow on us He then gave them their first task in spreading the Good News. They were not being commissioned to perform any miracles in His **name**; because they had already been doing that. He sends them forth to **forgive sin** and He showed them what that meant by His first words He spoke to them **'Peace be with you'**. He could have reminded them all of how they had turned away from Him, had failed Him in His hour of need but He doesn't, instead He says **'Peace'**. Earlier in St. John's Gospel we hear JESUS say: *'I have not come to condemn the world'* and again in the account of the woman caught in adultery He says to her, *'Does no one condemn you? Then neither do I.'*

JESUS shows that the way for the world to be healed is

through us using the wounds that others have inflicted on us and to turn them into the means by which we forgive them. The healing power of GOD is particularly powerful when, through the grace of GOD, we cry out, 'FATHER, forgive them for they know not what they do.'

We cannot do this in our own strength; we need all the gifts of the HOLY SPIRIT to help us to forgive as CHRIST has forgiven us.

His thirsting for us led to Him shedding His blood. His thirst cost Him His life.

When we pray 'Come down, O love divine', we will one day be asked to go beyond the point of only taking consolations from GOD too, when we are ready to share what He has given us with all whom we meet. The Dominican Motto is: 'Pass on to others the fruits of your contemplation.' JESUS says: *'You did not choose me, no I chose you, and I commissioned you to go out and bear fruit, fruit that will last.'*

The only fruit that we have that will last is CHRIST Himself. St. Peter meets the crippled man outside the Temple and says: *'I have no silver nor gold, but in the name of JESUS stand up.'* Who is GOD asking us to help 'stand up' by sharing with them the forgiveness that GOD has bestowed on us?

Are you a selfish Christian, only wanting CHRIST for yourself or are you self-less, eager to go out and fish for others, knowing that you of yourself have nothing to give, but in CHRIST JESUS you have, and you are, **everything**?

Do you now dare to join in with the composer and pray:

Come down, O love divine,
Seek thou this soul of mine,
And visit it with thine own ardour glowing;
O Comforter draw near,
Within my heart appear,
And kindle it, thy holy flame bestowing.

AMEN.

Note to Verse One:

8. Man was bound by the sin that He had committed and because of the first sin, Original Sin, all men were subject to death and futility. JESUS assumed our nature but He was without sin and He never sinned, but at the end of His life He took on our sin and died in it and then rose from the dead having dealt with the sin of all humanity.

Verse Two

O let it freely burn,
till earthly passions turn
to dust and ashes in its heat consuming;
and let thy glorious light
shine ever on my sight, and clothe me round,
the while my path illuming.

O let it freely burn

In the second verse the composer prays to deepen his faith. Having asked GOD that The Comforter would draw near he now asks that the fire of God's love would take full reign in his life and burn where it will.

This, is another line that is 'dangerous' for us to pray for ourselves because once we ask GOD to come and take possession of our hearts, minds and souls He will take our prayer seriously and remember that before the resurrection and the glory there is the cross. Therefore, once this line is prayed we need to be conscious that at some point in our lives we will identify, in a small way, CHRIST'S Passion and Death.

When GOD has free reign in us, that which in us that has already been configured to CHRIST will shine all the more brightly. As it shines more brightly though, it will shine up more and more the dark areas of our lives. Our wrong-doings and our wrong passions will be shown up for what they really are and it is at this point in the faith journey that many people despair and say that GOD has left them. They say that they once had a very close relationship with Him but now He seems to have gone from them and that He has not just left them but that He has left them in the dark.

If we think the same then we are not looking at our faith journey with the eyes of CHRIST, we are looking at faith through the eyes of the world. A world that screams at the top of its voice 'I want to have a perfect faith and I want it yesterday!' We are seeing faith with the world's view that everything is instant. To help us grow through this stage of wrong thinking we only have to contemplate that when

GOD became Incarnate, He did so as an embryo in the womb of the Virgin Mary. He came into this world as we came into this world and He went through the same stages of growth as we go through.

He did not jump from being an infant to being a man. He chose to be fully human and that meant He took on developing as we all have to. The WORD of GOD had to learn to form His letters and then from His letters to make words and from the words to make sentences. The Incarnate WORD of GOD had to learn to walk before He could learn to run. He had to learn how to form words before He could properly write and read. He had to go from being one to being two, from being two to being three and so on. He grew daily in exactly the same way as we do but in all He thought, said or did, He was without sin.

He read the Scriptures and began to understand that what He was reading or what He heard being read was about Himself. At every moment He, as we ourselves have, had the choice of whether to assent to what was being asked of Him by the FATHER or to ignore it. JESUS, the only begotten SON of GOD had come to fulfill the FATHER'S will and He never did anything, thought anything or spoke anything that was in discord with that will.

To ask the HOLY SPIRIT to burn freely within us is to pray a prayer that is beyond the first steps of the ladder of faith. Anyone who prays this prayer has moved on, as St. Paul would write, beyond drinking only milk, the food of babies, to feeding on something far more substantial and life changing, the WORD of GOD Himself.

When one reaches this stage in the spiritual journey it is no longer an exclusive relationship - something that is between you and GOD alone, but it is an inclusive relationship in which one is challenged to love not only GOD but your neighbour and yourself as well. At this point you are really living as a Christian rather than it being a faith that is purely for one's own salvation. Fr. William Hinnebush, O.P. writes in his book entitled *Renewal*, when speaking of the words of the Apostles when they justified the election of the seven deacons as these words having meaning for the lives of the Friars Preachers themselves and therefore would have meaning for all Christians: *'We will continue to devote ourselves to prayer and the service of the WORD'. (Acts 6: 4)* Prayer is needed, because the Gospel can only be proclaimed by those who have experienced it. The Gospel cannot be proclaimed by those who only know it: it can be experienced only in the loving dialogue of contemplative prayer. Dominican life is life in motion - a spiral motion constantly circling upward and outward. It surges up toward GOD; it leaps outward towards neighbour, it again springs upward towards Him. Its dynamic circling drives it eternally upward and outward. This is Dominican life.'[9]

This is indeed Dominican life but it is also a description of what the Christian life should be at its best. A life that is both **dynamic** and **eternal**. A life that **springs** forth from the source of all life which is CHRIST Himself for He describes himself as 'the LIFE'. To be caught up in the LIFE of CHRIST is to be caught up in the trinity and to be caught up in the lives of those around us.

If our **christian life** is other than **dynamic** and **eternal** then it is not really the fulness of the Christian life that we are living. But, I hear you shout loud and clear 'What about the times of spiritual darkness, the desert times, surely they are not dynamic; they are moments of incredible dryness and a sense of the absence of all that one has known of GOD up until now'. I challenge you to think about what you have said very carefully because even the 'driest' moment in our spiritual journey can be the source of deeper thirsting for that which is truth. It is a time of sifting out fact from fiction. The true doctrines of the faith from the falsehood that continues to buffet us on the wind from one corner to another. We begin to see Truth for Truth's sake and thus begin to live a life that is truly GOD centred, and if we are GOD centred we cannot be in anything that is dry or dead for GOD Himself is Eternal Life.

To say that GOD has brought me to the place of death is not a truth, because GOD will only draw us deeper and deeper into Himself, **life everlasting**.

Let me try and explain the point I am trying to make. In the Exodus account we are told of the moment in Chapter Three when Moses encounters 'I AM' at the Burning Bush and as he moves forward because he has been called by name: 'Moses, Moses,' we then hear a very clear instruction to Moses, 'Take off your shoes because you are on Holy Ground'. Gregory of Nyssa explains in his book on Moses, that GOD asks Moses to 'take off his shoes' because he is standing on Holy Ground and you can have nothing dead in the presence of the **living** GOD.

When Adam and Eve sin in the Garden they find themselves to be naked and GOD clothes them with 'animal skin'. This signifies that through their sin death entered their nature but this is changed by JESUS when He hangs on the cross because at that moment the SON of GOD and the Son of man is naked. HE literally clothed Himself not in a symbol of sin and death but actually took on Himself sin and death. Then when He died in His humanity He rose from the dead in the fulness of His humanity and His divinity, but what is important to realise is that where with Adam all men were clothed in death, through CHRIST man is now clothed in righteousness. CHRIST Himself restored man's justification with GOD. Therefore, if we are truly in CHRIST JESUS, then we too are clothed in His righteousness which means we can only move from life to life, even though we will all experience physical death. Thus, we cannot say that we are in a relationship with GOD that is bringing us into darkness and death. As Christians **we** are being brought all the while from darkness into light, from despair into joy, from death to life.

Let us remind ourselves of St. John's Gospel: *'He said to them, 'Peace be with you', and showed them His hands and His side. The disciples were filled with joy when they saw the LORD, and He said to them again, 'Peace be with you. As the FATHER sent Me, so I am sending you.' After saying this He breathed on them and said: 'Receive the HOLY SPIRIT, for those sins you forgive, they are forgiven: for those sins you retain, they are retained.' (John 20: 10-23)*

The HOLY SPIRIT, the love between the FATHER and the SON, is manifested by us in the love that we have for GOD, our neighbours and indeed in the love we show ourselves.

We are either living for GOD or we are holding out against

Him. We will find that as we grow in the things of GOD our spiritual selves and our flesh are increasingly at war with each other, with ever greater intensity. This is a movement from death to life not from life to death. We are being moulded ever more into His image and likeness. That which existed in humanity before the fall, once again has the chance to be. But once again the choice of life over death is ours. Let us in the power of the HOLY SPIRIT choose life at every turn.

St. Paul in his letter to the Romans expresses it this way: *'The unspiritual are interested only in what is unspiritual, but the spiritual are interested in spiritual things. It is death to limit oneself to what is unspiritual; life and peace can only come with concern for the spiritual. That is, to limit oneself to what is unspiritual is to be at emnity with GOD: such a limitation never could and never does submit to GOD'S law.'* (*Romans 8: 5f*)

He continues in verse 12: ... *'my brothers there is no necessity for us to obey our unspiritual selves or to live unspiritual lives. If you do live in that way you are doomed to die; but if by the SPIRIT you put an end to the misdeeds of the body you will live.'*

The composer chooses life over death because he gives the HOLY SPIRIT free reign in his life. This means that he is prepared then to take the good or the bad from GOD.

In this he echoes Job in the Old Testament: *'Job rose and tore his gown and shaved his head. Then falling to the ground he worshipped and said: 'Naked I came from my mother's womb, naked I shall return. YAHWEH gave, YAHWEH has taken back. Blessed be the name of YAHWEH!' (Job 1: 20-21)*

St. John would give us this word of advice: *'I am the true vine, and my FATHER is the vinedresser. Each branch in Me that bears no fruit He cuts away, and every branch that does bear fruit He prunes to make it bear even more. You are pruned already by means of the word that I have spoken to you. Make your home in Me, as I make mine in you. As a branch cannot bear fruit all by itself, but must remain a part of the vine, neither can you unless you remain in Me. I am the vine, you are the branches. Whoever remains in Me, with Me in Him, bears fruit in plenty; for cut off from Me you can do nothing. Anyone who does not remain in Me is like a branch that has been thrown away - he withers; these branches are collected and thrown in the fire, and they are burnt. If you remain in Me and My words remain in you you may ask what you will and you will get it. It is to the glory of My FATHER that you bear much fruit, And then you will be My disciples. As the FATHER has loved Me so have I loved you. Remain in My love.' (John 15: 1-9)*

These are words that we need to chew over and over again because each day they could all mean something entirely different than the day before. For example:

- Each branch in Me that bears no fruit He cuts away …
- Every branch that does bear fruit He prunes …
- You are pruned already … by the words I have spoken to you …
- Make your home in Me, as I make Mine in you …
- A branch cannot bear fruit all by itself …
- Whoever remains in Me … bears fruit in plenty
- Anyone who does not remain in Me … withers …
- If you remain in Me you will ask what you will and you will get it …
- As the FATHER has loved Me so I have loved you …
- Remain in My love…

If we were to take one phrase at a time and keep thinking about it, praying with it, chewing it over it would be enough material to feed our prayer for well over a year.[10]

When we give GOD free reign in us we are called to be grafted onto Him, the True Vine. If we are not grafted onto Him then we will be thrown into the refiner's fire. This fire is a fire to be afraid of because it will not bring life for us, but remember it is our choice to take this road to nowhere. John the Baptist warned the people of his time: *'Even now the axe is laid to the roots of the trees, so that any tree that fails to produce good fruit will be cut down and thrown into the fire. I baptise you with water for repentance, but the one who follows me is more powerful than I am, and I am not fit to carry His sandals; He will baptise you with the*

*HOLY SPIRIT and with **fire**. His winnowing-fan in His hand; He will clear His threshing floor and gather His wheat into the barn; but the chaff He will burn in a fire that will never go out.' (Matthew 3: 10-12)*

If we are thrown into a fire but we have given our lives over to GOD then we will not be harmed. Recall for a moment the three young men, Shadrach, Meshach and Abednego, who were thrown bound into the fiery furnace by King Nebuchadnezzar, and instead of being burnt to death they 'walked in the heart of the flames, praising GOD and blessing the LORD.' [11]

What, then, is the fire that we would wish to be thrown into? The fire that will never go out, or the **fire** of the HOLY SPIRIT which means being consumed by **love itself**? Once again the choice is ours. Will we remain standing after He has consumed us by **His love** or will we turn away, recoiling from a fire that will never go out? Once again, I repeat, the Good News is that the decision is ours to make. If we make a choice to be filled with the 'utter fulness of GOD' in the power of the HOLY SPIRIT then as we grow in GOD'S love there eventually is no choice because there is only one way to go. If one has an ounce of common sense we will choose to walk along the Way which by now we know is CHRIST Himself.

I urge you with all earnestness - choose **life**.

For many of us we need something tangible to happen to us before we make a decision of this kind. Many need 'proof' of GOD before they put their lives into His hands. St. Paul was one such person and his moment of 'conversion' came when he was literally blinded by **the light** on the road to Damascus. [12]

The disciples themselves, received at Pentecost what seemed like tongues of fire falling on their heads and they, like St. Paul, chose to respond and accept this incredible moment of grace, this amazing gift of **love** itself, of **life** itself.

Now, let us read what St. John has to say about the HOLY SPIRIT in his Gospel: *'I shall ask the FATHER and He shall send you another Advocate to be with you forever, the SPIRIT of TRUTH whom the world can never receive since it neither sees Him or knows Him; but you know Him, because He is with you, He is in you.'* (John 14:16)

When St. John comments that the world can never see the HOLY SPIRIT of GOD at work he is not talking about the world in general terms but about different individuals, some see Him and others do not. When St. Paul heard JESUS say to him on the road to Damascus, *'Saul, Saul, why are you persecuting me?'*, the people he was with saw

54

the same light as he did but they were not blinded by it, as he was for three days. Neither did they hear any voice. We can be in the midst of a great throng of people and yet be the only person to see the things of GOD.

When we experience the HOLY SPIRIT of GOD deep within our being we can try and try again to explain what we experience to members of our family, to friends, to work colleagues but if they have not had a similar experience it will only seem to them fanciful words. No matter how much we might want those who are closest to know GOD as we know Him we can never give them that experience of GOD, all we can do is create the setting but the response has to be their own. It is often the hardest part of giving our 'Yes' to GOD because we know that the outcome will probably be as He warns us in Scripture: that mother is divided against daughter, father against mother and so on.

The encouraging aspect of faith is that when it is the right time for us to say anything we will know what to say and how to say it because we are promised that the HOLY SPIRIT will guide us in all things: *'.. but the Advocate, the HOLY SPIRIT, whom the FATHER will send in My Name, will teach you everything and remind you of all I have said to you.'* *(John 14: 26)*

When the HOLY SPIRIT makes His home in us we find

ourselves responding to the graces of GOD in a new way. We have in ourselves a new sense of understanding of the mystery of GOD. We find ourselves thirsting for the things of GOD but find that when we 'drink from the well of salvation' the result is that we are hungrier than we were before we started and it seems that nothing can quench our thirst. It seems that the more we understand the more we don't know. Where we might have got frustrated in the past and prone to giving up early we find our desire to know increases. There is a new lightness in our spirit, a new hope, a new joy, a new sense of 'all will be well, all manner of things will be well'.

'When the Advocate comes, whom I shall send you from the FATHER, the SPIRIT of TRUTH who issues from the FATHER, He will be My witness.' (John 15: 26)

When we are blest with the HOLY SPIRIT we ourselves acquire a thirst for the **truth**, not only for the things of our faith but for all that we are involved in 'in the world.' An example of this is that if one works in an office one of the easiest things to do is to take the pen that you are given at work home with you; you put it in your pocket or bag at the end of the day. You don't give the pen another thought and it doesn't really matter if you do the same thing every day. Or another situation might be that we photocopy personal material on the work's photocopier during work time. Another example might be the copying of C.D's, or Audio Cassettes because we like the songs or the talks that are on them. All these things we never really give any thought to but when we are given the gift of the HOLY SPIRIT, the SPIRIT of TRUTH that issues from the FATHER, then we slowly begin to realise that each of these situations is wrong and we seek to change these habits that we have fallen into.

However, they have become habits and they don't go overnight. For a short period we manage to talk ourselves around the situation but deep down the understanding that these things are wrong keeps gnawing away at us until one day we ask for the strength to stop, not because of fear of 'getting caught one day' but because of **love**. We don't want to offend the one who loves us beyond our limitations and calls us into union with Himself. GOD is **love**. We have been made by GOD for love and to love. With the gift of the HOLY SPIRIT we see the things that block us from receiving that love and so we endeavour to stop what hinders us and turn to truth in all things and at all times, because we know that **love** itself has loved us. **Loved** us unto death.

If you find yourself with a few spare moments you might like to turn to John 16: 5-15 and ponder what it means for you. Remember, the choice is always yours!

Till earthly passions turn

St. Paul in his letter to the Ephesians writes: *'In particular, I want to urge you in the name of the LORD not to go on living the aimless kind of lives pagans live.'* (Ephesians 4: 17)

This is a real challenge to every person to think about how one speaks, acts and even thinks.

When GOD created us He made us then to be the 'Crown of His creation'. He had created everything and then He made man.

In the Genesis account the author tries to give us an image of a world being created from nothing and that it had all been created to support the life of man. 'Adam' meaning first man. After everything that GOD brings into being the author has GOD saying 'It is good' but after He has made man, He no longer says that His creation is good, but that it is 'very good.' In Psalm 8 we read:
'I look up at your heavens, made by your fingers,
at the moon and stars you set in place
- ah, what is man that you should spare a thought for him,
the son of man that you should care for him?
Yet you have made him little less than a god,
You have crowned him with glory and splendour,
made him lord over the works of your hands,
set all things under his feet ...'[13]

When we were created we were given a soul. This tremendous gift enables us to reason about our reason, in other words to think about our thinking. We have been created to be little less than a god but most of the time we never use our gift of reason.

For a greater part of our lives what we think, say or do is determined by what another does to us. We are not creative but reactive. When we are not creative but reactive we find that most of our life is consumed by defending ourselves and those we love, and this often leads to us being destructive rather than creative.

Many times in our lives we will either hear others say, or even say ourselves: 'Stop the world I want to get off!' Sadly, many do not come to the understanding that they have it within their own power to 'stop the world' and that is when we ourselves stop ourselves going from one thing to another with no thoughts in between. When we live like this we resemble animals rather that humans for they from the beginning do not possess that ability to reason about their reason.

Pause for a moment and see if what I have just said is true for you, it might not be so, but if it is see if any situation that you are in at the moment could be changed if you were only to take the time to think. As a child one of the lessons on teaching children about the highway code was to tell the children that when they reached a curb they should take a step back from the edge and stop for a moment and then look both ways and then to listen. If we were to apply this to our lives in general we might find that our quality of life improves tremendously and that that in itself improves the lives of those around us.

There are many things today that would turn our attention away from GOD but in truth man is only truly happy when he rests in GOD. The Catechism of the Catholic Church spells this out very plainly: 'The desire for GOD is written in the human heart, because man is created by GOD and for GOD; and GOD never ceases to draw man to Himself. Only in GOD will he find the truth and happiness he never stops searching for. The dignity of man rests above all on the fact that he is called to communion with GOD. This invitation to converse with GOD is addressed to man as soon as he comes into being. For if man exists it is because GOD has created him through love, and through love continues to hold him in existence. He cannot live fully according to truth unless he freely acknowledges that love and entrusts himself to his creator.' [14]

A little further on in the Catechism we read the following: 'Let the hearts of those who seek the LORD rejoice.' (Psalm 105: 3). Although man can forget GOD or reject Him, He never ceases to call every man to seek Him, so as to find life and happiness. But this search for GOD demands of man every effort of intellect, a sound will, 'an upright heart', as well as the witness of others who teach him to seek GOD. You are great, O LORD, and greatly to be praised: great is your power and your wisdom is without measure. And man, so small a part of your creation, wants to praise you: this man, clothed with mortality and bearing the evidence of sin and the proof that you withstand the proud. Despite everything, man, though a small part of your creation, wants to praise you. You yourself encourage him to delight in your praise, for you have made us for yourself, and our heart is restless until it rests in you.' [15]

St. Paul in his letter to the Colossians gives us all the guidance we need on how to live the Christian life. The question will be how eager are we to live by these guidelines or would we rather 'live in sin' because it is the easiest option now and I can think about the consequences of my actions tomorrow. The only problem with this way of life is that there might not be a 'tomorrow'. We need to remind ourselves again and again that everything we think, say or do has eternal consequences. We are always being asked, 'chose between life or death' but when we remind ourselves of this truth we need to remind ourselves that this decision will affect my life, and the lives of others now, but it always, as I have just stated, has eternal consequences. With this in mind let us heed what St. Paul has to say: *'Since you have been brought back to life with CHRIST, **you must look for the things that are in heaven,** where CHRIST is ......'*

'Let your thoughts be on heavenly things, not on the things that are on the earth, because you have died, and now the life you have is hidden with CHRIST in GOD. But when CHRIST is revealed ....you too will be revealed in all your glory with Him.'

'That is why you must kill everything in you that belongs only to earthly life: fornication, impurity, guilty passion, evil desires and especially greed, which is the same thing as worshipping a false god; all this is the sort of behaviour that makes GOD angry. And it is the way in which you used to live when you were surrounded by people doing the same thing, **but now, you of all people, must give up all these things:** getting angry, being bad-tempered, spitefulness, abusive language and dirty talk; and never tell each other lies.'

'You have stripped off your old behaviour with your old self, and you have put on a new self which will progress towards true knowledge the more that it is renewed in the image of its creator ...'

'You are GOD'S chosen race, his saints; HE loves you, and you should be clothed in sincere compassion, in kindness and humility, gentleness and patience. Bear with one another; forgive each other as soon as a quarrel begins. **The LORD has forgiven you: now you must do the same.** Over all these clothes, to keep them together and complete them, put on love. '[16]

62

'And may the peace of CHRIST reign in your hearts, because it is for this that you were called together as parts of the one body. Always be thankful.'

'Let the message of CHRIST, in all its richness, find a home with you. Teach each other, and advise each other, in all wisdom. With gratitude in your hearts sings psalms and hymns and inspired songs to GOD; and never say or do anything except in the name of the LORD JESUS, giving thanks to GOD the FATHER through Him.' (Colossians 3: 1-10,12-17)

There is so much in what St. Paul has written. It is hard to take it all in at one reading, try once again to both read the passage and pray through it taking one line at a time. There is ample material here for months of meditation, but whilst you meditate on the words remember the words of CHRIST: *'It is not enough to say LORD, LORD'*, … in order to get into the kingdom of GOD. What is required is that we make the WORD our home, 'not just listening and forgetting but actively putting it into practice'. Remember: 'Let the message in all its richness find a home with you.'

If we do these things then there is little danger of us ever falling away. The question that is constant for us all, constant in every choice that we have, every decision that we make is:

Are we going to be guided by
our earthly passions?

OR

Are we going to be guided by the
HOLY SPIRIT, the teacher of all truth?

The choice is ours. To help us to decide which way we
need to go in our decision making perhaps we need to ask
ourselves a more fundamental question :

How far do we want to go in our spiritual journey?

Or maybe it should be:

Do we want to take possession of the seats
that have been reserved for us in heaven?

Seats that have been bought and paid for
with the blood of JESUS our SAVIOUR.

Choose life or death!

To dust and ashes in its heat consuming

'You are GOD'S chosen race. You are HIS saints. The LORD has forgiven you. May the peace of CHRIST reign in your hearts. Let the message of CHRIST in all its richness find a home in you. GOD Himself has chosen you to be one of His saints.'

This is a very powerful statement that St. Paul makes but how do we hear it? Do we respond with: 'Oh that's nice but it doesn't apply to me, everyone else but not me, simply because I'm not good enough! ?

Or do we laugh at it with scorn because we don't believe it to be true and we laugh at anything to do with GOD all the time anyway?

Perhaps, though, perhaps you do believe it to be true, or at least hope it to be so, and so you take it to heart and allow it to affect the choices that you will make from now on.

St. Paul in his letter to the Ephesians writes: *'If we live by the truth and in love, we shall grow in all ways into CHRIST, who is the head by whom the whole body is fitted and joined together, every joint adding to its own strength, for each separated part to work according to its function. So the body grows until it has built itself up in love.'*

If we are to grow in love and allow CHRIST to form us and mould us there will come the point when we make a decision for ourselves that is wholly good. We make this choice of giving our lives over to CHRIST no matter what family, friends, neighbours, work-mates, school friends, or anyone else may think. We choose to live a life that is in **truth** and in **life**.

We make this choice because we understand that the more we allow ourselves to be consumed by perfect love, GOD - FATHER, SON and HOLY SPIRIT the more we will grow strong and firm. Our foundation will be CHRIST and we know that it is only in Him that we can 'live and move and have our being.'

We understand that with CHRIST as our foundation stone, our hidden selves will grow strong but only if CHRIST lives in our hearts through faith. We know that then, and only then, will we be planted in love and built on love. We will then long for the moment when, as St. Paul promises in his letter to the Ephesians: *'we will 'know' the love of CHRIST which is beyond all knowledge. Then, knowing the love of CHRIST which is beyond all knowledge, we will be filled with 'the utter fulness of GOD.'* *(Ephesians 3: 14-21)* (It is important to realise that the biblical meaning for 'know' is 'to experience'. Thus, in the context of St. Paul's letter we will not only 'know' about GOD but we will also 'experience' Him working in and through us. We will find ourselves saying and doing things that we once thought were way beyond our ability, and indeed still is, except that the grace of GOD working in our lives makes all things possible, because 'nothing is impossible for GOD' - as the angel Gabriel told Mary at the Annunciation in Luke 1: 38)

The question that we need to ask of ourselves is: How much of my life am I prepared to let GOD have control of'?

100%?

75%?

50%?

40%?

20%?

15%?

10%?

5%?

We really need to come to the understanding that it is only in that part of our lives that we have 'given over' to GOD that we will be '**fully alive**'. If we look at our choices coldly we will understand, by using simple mathematics, that we will only experience GOD in our lives if we have given Him over 50%. Any less than that will mean that our flesh is winning over our spiritual side simply because we choose to have it that way. If we haven't given GOD more than 50% of our lives then it will appear that GOD is 'not interested in us' and that 'He never answers our prayers'.

It is often said of GOD that He is 'a gentleman' in that He will never force us to do anything. He has given us the gift of 'Free Will' and He will never abuse that gift.

If you are someone who 'feels' that GOD is not interested in you, or that GOD never answers your prayers, take an honest look at yourself, your life-style and see how much you actually allow GOD to move in. If you do this little examination of one's life I am sure that you will quickly come to understand why it 'appears' that GOD is not interested in you or your prayers.

That part of your life that is not given over to GOD can only operate on the level of just 'merely existing' because it is only when we place ourselves in His care do we see how much He does care for us and those we care about.

The more we give our lives over to GOD the more we will find answers to those questions about life and death, peace and war, hatred and violence, justice and peace. The more we allow Him to guide our hearts and our minds the more we become informed, not just in the

literal sense of being formed in the mind but also in the
spiritual sense of being formed from within, in our souls
and hearts.

Another way of seeing how much of your life is given
over to GOD and that it is 'Fully Alive' is by looking at our
behaviour. I have already spoken at length about most of
our lives we are in reaction to what others say or do
around us or to us. If my 'reaction' is to respond in the
manner as I did when I was a child then I know that GOD
hasn't touched that part of my life yet because I would
not react like a child if I allowed Him to help me respond.
I am fully aware that JESUS invites us in the gospel to be
childlike so that we can enter heaven, but being child like
and childish are two very different things.

A few classic examples would be if as an adult we
understand something that is being done is negative. As
a child our reaction would have been to curl up into a
ball and suck one's thumb; withdrawing into a shell
remaining silent even though everyone else in a room is
talking normally; responding with anger which is out of
all proportion to the situation that you are in, even
throwing things. As a child we might have picked up the
nearest toy and thrown that in anger but as an adult we
don't throw the toys anymore, we go around slamming
doors and throwing the crockery. These may have been
appropriate behaviour patterns for the frightened child

but as an adult it becomes a barrier for ourselves against those around us. We know that GOD hasn't yet been 'invited into' those areas because He would not leave us as an adult with childish reactions.

As much as we grow physically we also need to grow emotionally and spiritually.

If we don't grow emotionally then when we hear the words of Sacred Scripture or hear what GOD can do, and has done, in other people's lives we will respond by either dismissing everything we see and hear 'in anger', screaming 'If only, you knew what happened to me then you wouldn't so readily say the things you do,' or, we may treat it with scorn and contempt, saying: 'That is for the weak-willed, it isn't for me; I don't need a comfort blanket ... I can get along all right by myself thank you very much!'

The healing of emotions can be very traumatic and needs to be done in an atmosphere of love and care and only working through different issues and situations as the person is able to respond.

If we are going to be 'fully alive in CHRIST JESUS' much of what we read in scripture will challenge us but we will discover that the situations and people that used to haunt us are no longer a problem. We find ourselves looking back and blinking because at the time of journeying with GOD in the healing of emotions and spiritual healing it seemed like an eternity. But when through it and out the 'other side' the journey suddenly seems as if it took no time and we wonder why we created all the fuss we did at the outset of the journey.

The past negativity will seem like dust and ashes round our feet. We will enjoy being who and what GOD had in mind from all eternity for us to be. We will accept, having gone through the refiner's fire, that we are one of GOD'S 'chosen race' one of His 'saints'.

All that I am saying simply boils down to freeing yourself in mind, heart and soul to 'become GOD-conscious' and thus seeing how simple and how blessed life can be. Rather than hiding in the corner we can't wait to 'Go out and share the Good News of what GOD has achieved in us'. St. Paul sums this up beautifully: '.. *so the saints together make a unity in the work of service, building up the body of CHRIST. In this way we all come to unity in our faith and in our knowledge of the SON of GOD, until we become the perfect* **man, fully mature** *with the fulness of CHRIST Himself.* **Then we shall not be children any longer** *and tossed one way or another and carried along by every wind of doctrine, at the mercy of all the tricks men play and their cleverness in practising deceit.' (Ephesians 4: 12-14)*

71

Let us then take full responsibility for ourselves, let us challenge ourselves to be totally grown up, to be **fully mature**. Let us bring all that is wrong in ourselves to the mercy of GOD that He might make good in us the Redemption that HE has won for us. Let us be 'fully alive in CHRIST JESUS', a 'living sacrifice of praise'.

And let thy glorious light

Let us not hesitate any longer, let us run into the **light**. Let us be blind and slow at responding to the graces that GOD wants to bestow on us no more.

'JESUS stopped and said: *'Call him here,'* So they called the blind man. *'Courage',* they said *'get up; He is calling you.'* So throwing off his cloak, (The Dominicans at the beginning of the Easter Gloria) he jumped up and went to JESUS. Then JESUS spoke, *'What do you want Me to do for you?* *'Rabbuni,'* the blind man said to Him, *'Master, let me see again.'* JESUS said to him, *'Go, your faith has saved you.'* And immediately his sight returned and he followed Him along the road.' (Mark 10: 49-52)

JESUS asked the blind man, *'What do you want Me to do for you?'* The blind man asks for sight and JESUS curing him says something which we need to notice. JESUS doesn't say, 'Go, your sight has returned!' No, He says, *'Go; your faith has saved you.'* JESUS cures the blind man enabling him to see again but the greatest thing he did for him was to enable him to grow in his spiritual journey. JESUS speaks the words of **salvation** … indeed, JESUS says *'Your faith has saved you'* implying not just an immediate healing but a healing that will spread into eternity.

JESUS asks us the same question: 'What do you want Me to do for you?' He wants us to take off the heavy cloaks that cover us and slow us down, our illness and all the things that other people would identify us as - the angry man, the selfish woman, etc. He wants us to cast off the works of darkness that we might experience the light and therefore be able to grow in our faith and knowledge of Him. To become His true disciples, as the blind man had become, for we read: *'and he followed Him along the road.'*

In Matthew 6: 22-23 we read: *'The lamp of the body is the eye. It follows that if your eye is sound, your whole body will be filled with light. But if your eye is diseased, your whole body will be all darkness. If then, the light inside you is darkness, what darkness will that be!'*

If this passage of scripture describes us in any way let us waste no time in 'throwing off' all that would cause us to remain blind. Let us waste no time in asking JESUS to show up the darkness of our lives that we might bring them to Him that He might heal us of them.

St. Paul writes very clearly on this subject: *'You were darkness once, but now you are light in the LORD. Be like children of light, for the effects of the light are seen in complete goodness right living and truth. Try to discover what the LORD wants of you, having nothing to do with the futile works of darkness but exposing them by contrast. The things that are done in secret are things that people are even ashamed to speak of; but anything exposed by the light will be illuminated and anything illuminated turns into light. That is why it is said: Wake from your sleep, rise from the dead, And CHRIST will shine on you. So be very careful about the sort of lives you lead, like intelligent and not like senseless people. This may be a wicked age, but your lives should redeem it. And do not be thoughtless but recognise what is the will of the LORD.'* (Ephesians 5: 7-17)

If only we would respond to these words of St. Paul, which are so clear. Then, not only will our lives take on a deeper understanding but we will have moved some way towards having 'the mind of CHRIST'. We will play our part in **salvation history**, our lives will become **REDEMPTIVE** by nature and **ESCATOLOGICAL** in its outlook.

St. Paul not only exhorted the Ephesians to be 'children of the light' but he asks the same thing in his letter to the Romans with a real sense of urgency: *'Besides, you know 'the time' has come: our salvation is even nearer to us now than* on the day when we were converted. The night is almost over, it will be daylight soon - let us give up the things we do under cover of dark; let us arm ourselves and appear in the light. Let us live decently as people do in the daytime: no orgies, no promiscuity or licentiousness, and no wrangling or jealousy. Let your armour be the LORD JESUS CHRIST; forget about satisfying your bodies with all their cravings.' (Romans 13: 11-14)

Let us take the promptings of St. Paul to heart and once again not just read it, but think and pray through the words until we 'become what we pray' - true children of the light. Let us live as if the **light** of CHRIST is shining on us all the time, but it is only that we can't see it because we cover ourselves with the things of this world. Indeed if we find ourselves in a darkened room and someone suddenly puts the full light on we cry out instantly 'put out the light!' Let us earnestly seek never to put out or dim the **light** which is CHRIST JESUS our LORD and SAVIOUR..

Shine ever on my sight

When we turn our minds to CHRIST JESUS and heed what He says to us through Sacred Scripture, the Tradition of the Church, the Magisterium and the Papal Encyclicals, we will discover that the things of the world that were once so important to us no longer bear the same significance in our lives. We literally begin to see and experience things in a new light. Everything, no matter how hard it seems at the time, when seen through the **light** of CHRIST takes on a positive meaning. Everything is seen as it should be. We begin to see the Sacred all around us. We also begin to see that which is dark within us and around us and as much as we are transfigured by the **light** we see and experience how awful are the works that are done in the darkness including our own sins.

When we see people and situations through the **light** of CHRIST nothing anymore is seen to be beyond Redemption, no effort on our part ever seems futile because we see everything as CHRIST would want us to see it. This is true for the tiniest grain of sand on the shore and for our long standing problems in relationships and long standing health issues.

Let us take a quick glance through Sacred Scripture to see where the **light** of CHRIST changes even the hardest of moments, including death, into a time of great joy.

A - The Transfiguration: (Matthew 17: 1-8)
'Six days later, JESUS took with Him Peter and James and his brother John and led them up a high mountain where they could be alone. There in their presence He was transfigured: His face shone like the sun and His clothes became as white as

76

light. Suddenly Moses and Elijah appeared to them; they were talking with Him ... ... He was speaking when suddenly a bright cloud covered them with its shadow, and from the cloud there came a voice ...'

Recall to mind the Genesis account of the beginning of creation. The HOLY SPIRIT hovered over the formless void and then GOD spoke a Word and then there was **light** ... He hovered over Mary and covered her with His shadow ... He hovered over the void of Her womb and she conceived the LIGHT, the WORD of GOD Himself. Whenever the HOLY SPIRIT, or a cloud, hovers in scripture it is usually a sign of the mighty works that GOD is about to work. GOD is making a statement ... He is teaching us and through these manifestations He always invites us into an ever deeper relationship with Himself. GOD actually tells us what the 'theophany' of the cloud means when He speaks with Moses at the Burning Bush:

B - The Encounter Between YAHWEH and Moses on Mount Sinai: (Exodus 19:9)

'YAHWEH said to Moses, 'I am coming to you in a dense cloud so that the people may hear when I speak to you and may trust you always.'

C - The Crucifixion: Luke 23: 39-43

'You got the same sentence as He did, but in our case we deserved it: we are paying for what we did but this man has done

nothing wrong. 'JESUS,' he said 'remember me when you come into your kingdom.'

JESUS had promised, *'When I am lifted up I shall draw all men to myself.'* His first 'lifting' was on Mount Tabor, His crucifixion was His second. Here there was no blinding light, no theophany, indeed it was a completely opposite scene that engulfed the three crosses on the hill of Golgotha, the place of the skull, everything turned black as JESUS was dying on the cross. A silent stillness all about but although one could hardly see in front of you for those who had searched the bottom of their hearts for understanding and forgiveness there came for them a blinding light of inward illumination transforming their minds and their souls. The 'good thief" was one of the few at the crucifixion, of the SON of GOD, who experienced this light. Can you recall in Verse One when JESUS came to His disciples in the dark, walking on the water through the storm? At the crucifixion JESUS does the same for this thief who was in his own darkest hour. Whilst JESUS hangs on the cross He consoles the thief and at the same time gives witness once more to the FATHER, showing for the last time what He meant when He said He had come to fulfill the FATHER'S will and not His own. Through the conversion of the thief the FATHER is glorified.

D - The Ascension: (Acts1: 9-11; Luke 24: 3-6; Luke 24: 31)

'As He said this He was lifted up while they looked on, and a cloud took Him from their sight.'

At this moment the disciples witnessed what was in store for themselves and for anyone else who is in CHRIST JESUS. They looked up and saw their destiny and ours.

'As they stood there not knowing what to think, two men in brilliant clothes suddenly appeared at their side. Terrified, the women lowered their eyes. But the two men said to them, 'Why look among the dead for someone who is alive?'

This extract poses a question for us: 'Are we like the women looking in the wrong place to find life - the life to the full that JESUS promised us? Are we looking too much at the past and failing to notice, quite literally, that life has passed on? Have we come to a standpoint where we are bound by the past and afraid of the future?

Are we terrified to follow CHRIST totally?

Are we seeking guidance from the right people in the things of life and of faith, people who hold us back from moving forward simply because they themselves don't know the way because they are living off their past experiences rather than the GOD of now, 'I AM who AM'?

'And their eyes were opened and they recognised Him; but

He had vanished from their sight. Then they said to each other 'did not our hearts burn within us as He talked to us on the road and explained the Scriptures to us'?

The two disciples could say that their hearts burnt within them when JESUS explained the Scriptures to them, when was the last time that we could say that our hearts also burnt when we were reading Sacred Scripture? When was the last time that we prayed and asked the HOLY SPIRIT to come and illuminate our minds that we might fully understand what we read or hear what is proclaimed? When, if ever, has anything of GOD made us feel as if our hearts were burning?

Ask the HOLY SPIRIT to guide you as you read and contemplate the mysteries of GOD in Scripture or during a prayer: whilst you pray the Rosary or celebrate the Holy Sacrifice of the Mass with members of the Mystical Body of CHRIST.

E - The Stoning of St. Stephen: (Acts 8: 55-58)

'But, Stephen filled with the HOLY SPIRIT, gazed into heaven and saw the glory of GOD, and JESUS standing at GOD'S right hand.'

When JESUS rose from the dead and ascended into heaven the gates of heaven were 'opened' and they have never been closed again. When we find life to be too much of a struggle ask GOD to send you consolation through His angels and saints, you might not see them but you will know that they are with you to guide you, to bless you and to protect you. When, if ever, was the last time you asked your Guardian Angel to help you?

I hear you complain and say 'But the Church stopped teaching about angels with the Second Vatican Council, the Church 'threw out angels and they stopped teaching about Purgatory and Hell at the same time.' That might be what you heard but it has to be said that the Church continues to teach us about these in the new Catholic Catechism. (I invite you to pick up your copy and look these things up because then you will see for yourselves what the Church does actually teach rather than basing your belief on what other people think. If you don't own one I would go so far as to encourage you to buy a copy of your own because it is absolutely fascinating! Don't be put off by the size of the book; it is quite easy to read because it has been so well set out and it has been compiled from a wonderful range of sources.)

F - The Conversion of Saul: (Acts 9:1-12)
'Suddenly, while he was travelling to Damascus and just before he reached the city, there came a light from heaven all round him. He fell to the ground, and then he heard a voice saying, 'Saul, Saul, why are you persecuting me?
When have we heard the voice of the LORD calling out to us, as clearly as Saul heard it, and stopping us in our tracks? It is so important in the spiritual journey to take

time to reflect on our lives every now and again. This can be done by:

• Making an examination of conscience each night whereby we run through the events of the day in our minds and see where we have allowed ourselves to be guided by GOD and where we have raced on ahead of him and fallen down in our tracks.

• Going to the Sacrament of Penance (otherwise known as Reconciliation or Confession) and before we go to take a passage of scripture like 1 Corinthians 13: 1-13. Read it through and ask GOD to highlight the sins that you have committed that need His grace and His mercy so that you can be freed from the effects of those sins on yourself and the other members of the Mystical Body of CHRIST - the Church.

• Every day taking a passage from Sacred Scripture and either read it, pray through it - putting yourself in the scene that you are reading about and respond as if GOD Himself was challenging you or encouraging you (which is of course what is happening because Sacred Scripture is the **living** WORD of GOD that 'cuts more finely than any double edged sword.)

• Attending the Holy Sacrifice of the Mass as often as you can in a week, because we are participating fully in the one **Life, Death, Resurrection and Ascension of** CHRIST. The Holy Sacrifice of the Mass is the greatest prayer that we can pray because it is the one prayer that quite literally leads us into **communion with** GOD, which is the aim of the spiritual life. The Holy Sacrifice of the Mass is the closest we can get in our life-time to experiencing a real taste of heaven on earth. Remember that the psalmist invites us to, *'Taste and See that the LORD is good'.*

So, I repeat, when was the last time you heard the LORD speaking to you and calling you ever deeper into Himself? When has your heart burnt within you? When was the last time your heart missed a beat because GOD Himself had touched your life and made your burden lighter?

And clothe me round the while my path illuming

We read in the first chapter of St. Luke's Gospel: *'The HOLY SPIRIT will come on you and the power of the MOST HIGH will overshadow you.' (Luke 1: 35-36)* How open are we to receive the gifts that GOD wants to give us, not least His own power in the HOLY SPIRIT? How open are we in receiving His grace and His mercy, especially when we recall the words of St. Thomas Aquinas: 'One drop of supernatural grace is greater than the whole of the created order'? Are our eyes shut, our ears gone deaf and our hearts grown cold because we are not only looking for 'life among the dead' but without realising it we have become dead, empty, cold and hard hearted.

The prophet Ezekiel prophesied as follows: *'The hand of Yahweh was laid on me, and He carried me away by the spirit of YAHWEH and set me down in the middle of a valley; a valley full of bones. He made me walk up and down them. There were vast quantities of these bones on the ground the whole length of the valley; and they were quite dried up. He said to me, 'Son of man, can these bones live?' I said, 'You know, LORD YAHWEH'. He said, prophesy over these bones. Say, 'Dry bones, hear the word of YAHWEH. The LORD YAHWEH says this to these bones: I am now going to make the breath enter you, and you will live. I shall put sinews on you, I shall make flesh grow on you, I shall cover you with skin and give you breath, and you will live; and you will learn that I am YAHWEH.' I prophesied as I had been ordered. While I was prophesying, there was a noise, a sound of clattering; and the bones joined together. I looked, and saw that they were covered with sinews; flesh was growing on them and skin was covering them, but there was no breath in them. He said to me, 'Prophesy to the breath; prophesy, son of man. Say to the breath, 'The Lord Yahweh says this: Come from the four winds, breath; breathe on these dead; let them live! I prophesied as He had ordered me, and the breath entered them; they came to life again and stood up on their feet, a great immense army.*

'Then He said, 'Son of man, these bones are the whole House of Israel. They keep saying, 'Our bones are dried up, our hope has gone; we are as good as dead.' So, prophesy. Say to them, 'The LORD YAHWEH says this: 'I am now going to open your graves; I mean to raise you from your graves, My people, and lead you back to the soil of Israel. And you will know that I am YAHWEH, when I open your graves and raise you from your graves, My people. And I shall put My SPIRIT in you, and you will live, and I shall resettle you on your own soil; and you will know that I, YAHWEH, have said and done this - it is the LORD YAHWEH who speaks.' (Ezekiel 37: 1-14)

Where Ezekiel speaks of the 'dry bones' and the 'House of Israel' we can substitute our own names into the text at those places and when we personalise Sacred Scripture in this way it takes on a whole different meaning.

As we grow older or become used to the way that GOD works in our lives our senses can become dulled. Without realising it we do become like the 'dry bones' of Ezekiel and when this happens only one thing can bring us 'back to life' and that is the breath of GOD, the HOLY SPIRIT - the same breath that was given to Adam which made him into a living being.

Sometimes, we become dull to the things of GOD because

we have been called to a position in the Church i.e. Reader, Eucharistic Minister. When we were initially invited to these positions we were humbled and excited at the same time. We developed a new sense of 'wonder and awe in GOD'S presence' but as the weeks moved into months and months moved into years that initial 'feeling' wore off.

This is wonderfully depicted in 1 Samuel 3: 1-8: *'Now the boy Samuel was ministering to YAHWEH in the presence of Eli (the priest); it was rare for YAHWEH to speak in those days; visions were uncommon. One day, it happened that Eli was lying down in his room. His eyes were beginning to grow dim; he could no longer see. The lamp of GOD had not yet gone out, and Samuel was lying in the sanctuary of YAHWEH where the ark of GOD was, when YAHWEH called, 'Samuel! Samuel!' He answered, 'Here I am'. Then he ran to Eli and said, 'Here I am, since you called me'. Eli said, 'I did not call. Go back and lie down.' So he went and lay down. Once again YAHWEH called, 'Samuel! Samuel!' Samuel got up and went to Eli and said, 'Here I am, since you called me'. He replied, 'I did not call you, my son; go back and lie down'. Samuel had as yet no knowledge of YAHWEH and the word of YAHWEH had not yet been revealed to him. Once again YAHWEH called, the third time. He got up and went to Eli and said, 'Here I am, since you called me'. Eli then understood that it was YAHWEH who was calling the boy, and he said to Samuel, 'Go and lie down, and if someone calls say, 'Speak, YAHWEH, your servant is listening.' So Samuel went and lay down in his place.'*

The LORD, YAHWEH, does call Samuel again and he gives him a message for Eli. Eli, the priest had let his heart grow cold to the point of not even bothering to correct his own sons when they cursed YAHWEH. Samuel is young and at the beginning of a tremendous relationship with YAHWEH which would last for many years, a relationship that Samuel never let 'grow cold'. From this account we can understand that if we don't keep listening for the voice of YAHWEH in our every day circumstances our hearts cannot but grow cold because the HOLY SPIRIT would not be active in them. Many people are baptised into the FATHER, SON and HOLY SPIRIT. They have more than 'one drop of supernatural grace' in them.

GOD Himself comes and makes His home in them but because they have never been in a place or with people who are 'GOD conscious' their living faith is never encouraged to grow. Once a person has been baptised it can never be erased or 'taken back'. It is a gift from GOD to be with the person for all time and it wakens their souls to eternal life with GOD.

Spend some time pondering the two texts of Sacred Scripture that I have quoted in this section and ask yourself the question, answering as honestly as you can: 'Has your relationship with the **living** GOD developed much since you were baptised, or when you were a child, has your faith gone stale? If it has, now is the opportunity to ask the HOLY SPIRIT to breathe on you once again that you might know and experience to the full 'the wonder and awe in GOD'S presence'. If your relationship with GOD has developed as you have developed then I invite you to still do the exercise that I give you, that GOD might manifest Himself to you in ever increasing depths of love.

I invite you to find a quiet point in the day, sit yourself in a comfortable seat and then first read the prayer that follows and then when you are 'ready' take the time to pray each line very slowly. Don't rush, there is no need to hurry this, if you have picked the right time. Do not try and pray this with one eye on the clock because you are waiting for someone to arrive or because someone might come in and 'catch you being holy' because 'you' will get in the way of your own prayer.

A NOVENA TO THE HOLY SPIRIT

(Preferably prayed nine days in a row ...
but every day for the rest of your life
would be good as well!)

Come, O HOLY SPIRIT, come, and from your
celestial home, send your rays of light divine.

Come, O FATHER of the poor; come, with treasure
that endures; come, within our poor hearts shine.

You, of all consolers best, and the soul's most
welcome guest; Your refreshing peace bestow.

Perfect rest in toilsome task; in the heat Your breath
we ask; solace in the midst of woe.

Light Immortal! Light Divine! In our hearts let
Your light shine; and our inmost being fill.

If You take Your grace away; nothing good in man
can stay. All his good is turned to ill.

continued ....

..... Novena continued

Heal our wounds, our strength renew; on our dryness pour Your dew; wash the stains of guilt away.

Bend the stubborn heart and will; melt the frozen, warm the chill; guide the steps that go astray.

LORD, on those who ever more, You confess and You adore; in Your sevenfold gifts descend.

Give them virtue's sure reward; give them Your salvation, LORD; Give them joys that never end.

Amen, Alleluia.

**May you come to know the
'utter fulness of GOD'**

*Come down, O love divine,
seek thou this soul of mine
and kindle it, thy holy flame bestowing.*

Notes to Verse Two:
9. Renewal in the Spirit of St. Dominic, William Hinnebush, O.P. pages 7-8
10. This way of praying is a method used by the monks of many years ago and is still used today. It is called 'Lectio Divina'.
11. Daniel 3: 23-24.
12.. JESUS refers to Himself as the Light of the World, see John 7:12
13. Psalm 8:3-6
14. Paragraph 27, page 14. Quote: Vatican Council II 'Gaudium et spes', 7 Dec 1965, paragraph 19.1.
15. Paragraph 30, page 15. Quote: St. Augustine's Confessions.
16. cf. 1 Corinthians 13: 1-13.

Verse Three

Let holy charity mine outward vesture be,
And lowliness mine inner clothing;
True lowliness of heart,
Which takes the humbler part,
And o'er its own shortcomings
Weeps with loathing.

Let holy charity mine outward vesture be

1 Corinthians 13: 1-13 says: *'If I have all the eloquence of men or of angels, but speak without love, I am simply a gong booming or a cymbal clashing. If I have the gift of prophecy, understanding all the mysteries there are, and knowing everything, and if I have the faith in all its fulness, to move mountains, but without love, then I am nothing at all. If I give away all that I possess, piece by piece, and if I even let them take my body to burn it, but am without love, it will do me no good whatever. Love is always patient and kind; it is never jealous; love is never boastful or conceited; it is never rude or selfish; it does not take offence, and is not resentful. Love takes no pleasure in other people's sins but delights in the truth; it is always ready to excuse, to trust, to hope, and to endure whatever comes.*

'Love does not come to an end. But if there are gifts of prophecy, the time will come when they must fail; or the gift of languages, it will not continue forever; and knowledge - for this, too, the time will come when it must fail. For our knowledge is imperfect and our prophesying is imperfect; but once perfection comes, all imperfect things will disappear. When I was a child, I used to talk like a child, and think like a child, and argue like a child, but now I am a man, all childish ways are put behind me. Now we are seeing a dim reflection in a mirror; but then we shall be seeing face to face.

'The knowledge that I have now is imperfect; but then I shall know as fully as I am known. In short, there are three things that last: faith, hope and love; and the greatest of these is love.'

1 Corinthians 13: 1-13 is one of the most well known

passages of Scripture. It is read at most weddings and indeed often at the taking of religious vows or at priestly ordination. But, although the words are very well known for the most part this passage is for the majority who would quote it only that - well known words. However, for the serious Christian these words present a tremendous challenge. The challenge is that we would become the very words we read, that we would:

• always speak with love

• ensure that every single action that we would do, no matter how great or small it would be, would be firmly rooted in love.

• always be patient and kind

• never be jealous; boastful; conceited; rude; selfish; take offence at what is said or done to us and never be resentful …… under any circumstance.

• never take pleasure in other people's sins - and would

• always trust; excuse; hope and endure whatever comes our way … for good or ill.

Just think for a moment about your life and see if there have ever been moments when you have taken offence at anything or indeed at anyone.

Has there been a moment in your life when for a brief period you have been upset about what other people have said or done either to yourselves or to someone else?

Maybe there have been times when people have criticised the way you speak, the way you walk, the way you look, your intelligence and in being criticised you have been hurt deeply.

Perhaps when you think of such occasions they might be, for you, times when you actually justify your dislike of another or indeed justify your bitterness towards them because, after all they are the ones who have hurt you.

St. Paul would encourage us, however, that even in such times as these, there can be no justification to desist from loving.

If CHRIST'S love truly reigns in our hearts then when these times are recalled by us we would, in the power of the HOLY SPIRIT, have the strength to love others as He loved us and pray for those who have hurt us, as He did for us on the cross, 'FATHER, forgive them for they know not what they do'.

Indeed, if we were really living out of the **redemptive**

love of CHRIST we would instead of condemning people for the pain that they have caused us, search for a way in which to excuse them of their behaviour.

This is not an easy thing to be able to do and that is why I speak of achieving such a tremendous goal only through the power of the HOLY SPIRIT.[17]   The same HOLY SPIRIT that enabled JESUS to follow through and carry out His FATHER'S will and love us unto death, death on a cross.

On an encouraging note, remember that at all times there are people watching to see what we would do; how we behave in situations that are particularly hard. Through our being able to co-operate with the gift of grace they might be encouraged to respond to the gift of grace themselves and thus be set free from being bound up by unforgiveness.

We are only able to live the words of this passage if we have indeed already progressed through verses one and two of this hymn. In fact, if we can actually live the words of the first two verses of this hymn this scripture verse would indeed be an apt description of us. Let us for a moment remind ourselves of the first two verses:

Come down, O love divine,
Seek thou this soul of mine,
And visit it with thine own ardour glowing;
O Comforter, draw near,
Within my heart appear,
And kindle it, thy holy flame bestowing.

O let it freely burn,
Till earthly passions turn
To dust and ashes in its heat consuming;
And let thy glorious light
Shine ever on my sight, and clothe me round,
The while my path illuming.

Examination of Conscience:

In your mind take yourself back over the past week and examine your thoughts, words and deeds. Recall also the times that you had an opportunity to do something and chose not to respond to the prompting of the HOLY SPIRIT (known as the sins of **omission**), and see if there were occasions when you could have loved GOD, another, and yourself, more than you actually did. If there are any such times ask the LORD to give you the grace to respond to the same situation, if it happens in the future, in a more loving way. If you find that prayer too hard then begin by asking the LORD to give you the grace of the **desire** to love and to forgive those who have hurt you or may be hurting you in the present.[18]

If you find this step hard then perhaps it might be a good step to take a crucifix off the wall, if you have one. If you don't possess one you might consider buying one. Hold it in your hands and ask GOD for the grace to understand the love that He has for you and to show you the times that He has forgiven you your acts that have caused others to suffer in some way or other.[19] As He forgives you may you then receive the grace to forgive others as He has forgiven you in CHRIST JESUS, His SON. [20]

And lowliness become mine inner clothing

The Catechism of the Catholic Church states in paragraph 2559: '... when we pray, do we speak from the height of our pride and will, or 'out of the depths of a humbled and contrite heart'? .... Humility is the foundation of prayer.' and concludes with a quote from St. Augustine: 'Man is a beggar before GOD.'

I am quite sure that for the most part many of us will say that this is of course the attitude that we adopt whilst praying, for it is in prayer that we know that we are indeed nothing and GOD is everything. This is true even if our prayer consists only of prayers of request or the prayers of bargaining with GOD; i.e:

Dear GOD,
I come before you knowing that you are my GOD and that in you all things are possible. I pray that you would enable me to get this new job that is coming up. If I get it LORD I promise to pray an extra Hail Mary every night. Thank you.   **Amen!**

In prayer, as I have just said, we might be truly humble. The question that raises itself when we speak of a state of true humility is, 'Are we humble when it comes to our attitude to other people, especially those who are younger than us; less experienced; less educated; less good looking; less .... ?' I could go on with this list for a long time.

Are we people who always want to be 'on the top'? A simple illustration that comes to mind is one of a family with three young children. The eldest is extremely bright, as in fact are all the children, and they are playing a competitive game. The eldest child wins with little effort every time when finally an encouraging parent, wishing to teach the child something of humility, says to their eldest as they draw them to one side so that the other children are out of earshot: 'How about letting your brothers win for a change.' The oldest child replies in shock: 'but, daddy, you couldn't possibly want me to lose on purpose, could you, and not show how good I am?'

The parent in this case will know that they will have to wait for another opportunity to show their eldest that life is not always about coming out on top, even if you have the necessary gifts to be able to do so.

Examination of Conscience:

Think about the times in the last month when you may have had the opportunity to allow another to 'shine' instead of yourself. See if on each opportunity you, in true humility, allowed the other to shine or did you want to try to appear to be the best in the given situation?

If it is the case that you didn't want others to appear better than yourself, you might like to recall each situation. Look at your relationship with the person or persons in question and ask yourself very honestly why it was that you couldn't allow them to be better than you. Often, the answer will be because we ourselves actually lack confidence and in some way are insecure in ourselves. For if we are truly content with ourselves we will have no problem allowing other people to be seen to be better than we are.

Read through and slowly reflect on the words of Psalm 131:
'Yahweh, my heart has no lofty ambitions,
My eyes do not look too high.
I am not concerned with great affairs
Or marvels beyond my scope.
Enough for me to keep my soul tranquil and quiet
Like a child in its mother's arms,
As content as a child that has been weaned.'

Ask yourself if you have any lofty ambitions that get in the way of you enjoying life to the full because the ambition has made you too competitive to be able to enjoy the giftedness of another.

See if in all situations of life you would rather hold on to peace and tranquility than get caught up in what has commonly become known as 'the Rat Race'.

Take a look at all your relationships and see if in each one of them the underlying factor is one of love and contentment. If you find that this is not so, take a deeper look at that particular relationship and see if there is anything you can do to bring about a more tranquil situation. For instance, is there any area of the relationship in which you find you have become entrenched and are digging your heels in deeper and deeper making a firm stand for your own wants and desires. See if in this situation you could actually 'die to self' and allow the other the opportunity for them to have their desires fulfilled. This might seem a very hard thing to do but as the Gospel would tell us, it is much better to give than to receive, especially if what we want causes another pain and anguish.

True lowliness of heart

Sometimes being very honest about our own limitations can be a very hard thing to admit to ourselves let alone anyone else. However, if we are to become the person that GOD wants us to be and that is a true image of Himself then there are times that we need to admit to our limitations in order to allow GOD to give us the gift of grace that will enable us, and consequently those around us, to grow.

Moses is one of the most famous of Biblical characters. There is the incredible account in Exodus when Moses meets the LORD, I AM WHO AM, at the Burning Bush. As you know, during this encounter Moses is asked by GOD to go to Pharaoh, King of Egypt, and ask that the Israelites be set free from their bondage to slavery. During the conversation many things pass between GOD and Moses including GOD giving Moses two signs in order to show Moses that GOD was GOD and that if Moses went in His name all things would be possible. However, it is not until the very end of the episode that Moses actually expresses to GOD what is bothering him.

In Exodus 4:10-17 we read: *'Moses said to YAHWEH, 'But, my LORD, never in my life have I been a man of eloquence, either before or since you have spoken to your servant. I am a slow speaker and not able to speak well.' 'Who gave man his mouth?' YAHWEH answered him. 'Who makes him dumb or deaf, gives him sight or leaves him blind? Is it not I, YAHWEH? Now go, I shall help you to speak and tell you what to say.' 'If it please you, my LORD,' Moses replied 'send anyone you will!' At this the anger of YAHWEH blazed out against Moses, and he said to him, 'There is your brother Aaron the Levite, is there not? I know that he is a good speaker. Here he comes to meet you. When he sees you his heart will be full of joy. You will speak to him and tell him what message to give. I shall help you to speak, and him too, and instruct you what to do. He himself is to speak to the people in your place; he will be your mouthpiece, and you will be as the god inspiring him.'*

Moses had been having a conversation with GOD but only at this point does Moses actually admit to GOD what it is that is wrong. We can surely understand GOD'S frustration at this point in the episode. HE had been so patient with Moses but in spite of everything GOD had said or done to help Moses with the mission that he was being entrusted with, Moses kept on coming up with more and more problems. It is only at the end that he admitted to the fact that the problem was actually his own inadequacy of speech.

What had prevented Moses from speaking the truth to GOD before? Fear? I don't think so because he had been engaged in this amazing conversation for such a long time. Indeed, if Moses had been afraid of GOD he would not have reached the point of taking off his shoes which enabled him to move closer and become more intimate with the one who was speaking to him.

Perhaps the answer is a lot simpler: perhaps it was Moses' pride that was getting in the way. You ask, 'How can it be pride if one is afraid of admitting what one cannot do'. It is pride whenever we fail to admit who and what we really are. We try and carry on with a brave face trying to prevent people from knowing our true weaknesses – this is indeed pride.
We are invited by GOD to always have lowliness of heart and that means that we should neither be puffed up with

our own self importance or trying to hide the weaknesses that we know we have.

GOD invites us always to allow Him to be GOD in our lives and that means that we are honest with Him. Remember He already knows us and in knowing us, with all our defects, He calls us to follow Him. To do, as our Holy Mother Mary would say, *'Whatever He tells you.'*

GOD invites us to allow Him to equip us for those tasks that He has called us to. For GOD never calls without equipping. We only need to look at the Sacramental life of the Church to see that this is true. For in His Sacramental life He feeds us with His own Body and Blood. In Baptism He brings us through death to life in Him. In Confirmation He gifts us the Advocate, the HOLY SPIRIT the one who will teach us all things and lead us into the truth of all things, especially sin.

So, we often get it wrong. So often we understand the call of GOD but then we either become proud because of the reality that GOD has called us and as a consequence we belittle those around us. Or, in recognising our call we think it is because of our own giftedness that we have been called and that we do not need GOD once we have responded to that initial invitation.

GOD calls every person to live a life of holiness. In fact, St. Paul writes in his epistle to the Ephesians: *'Before the world was made he chose us, chose us in Christ to be holy and spotless and to live through love in his presence.' It is all GOD'S doing: His invitation; His Blessing; His gifting; and His enabling us to 'live through love in His presence'.* If we come to understand this then we will want to serve Him because of love and out of love not out of any desire to boast or to be raised higher than anyone else. In fact if we truly understand the nature of our call we will recognise that we are only to follow in the steps of the SON and that means to 'serve and not to be served'.

In the area of service there is plenty of opportunity for 'lowliness of heart'. All we have to do is 'die to self' in order to lift another higher.

Take some time to look at the different areas of your life and see if in each one of them you can honestly say that you want the whole-hearted good of the other. That in all things you would rather serve than 'be served'.

Take a moment to also look at your life and see if you freely accept any limitations that you might have, giving them over to GOD that He might be glorified through them and in them. These can be physical disabilities, ill health, emotional disabilities stemming from our character or because we have in some way been hurt emotionally.

It is important to always recall these words: *'GOD works all things to good for those who love Him.'* If we do indeed love Him then even our 'limitations' will become a source of strength for us in the service of GOD and our neighbour.

Pray at all times and in all places that everything in your life will be used for the greater glory of GOD. If you can do this then there will be little chance of you ever becoming proud and instead you will steadily take on the countenance of one who is truly 'lowly in heart'.

Which takes the humbler part

Have you ever stopped to ponder the beginning of the second chapter of St. Paul's Epistle to the Philippians? I would like us to begin this section with his words because they are such a wonderful song of praise to the humility of the SON of GOD himself:

'In your minds you must be the same as CHRIST JESUS:
His state was divine,
yet he did not cling
to his equality with GOD
but emptied himself

to assume the condition of a slave,
and became as men are;
and being as all men are,
he was humbler yet,
even to accepting death,
death on a cross.'   (Philippians 2: 5-8)

What an invitation St. Paul gives us or indeed what a challenge for us to respond to with all our minds, hearts, souls and bodies, for this is truly a challenge for us to give all that we have and are over to GOD.

'In your minds you must be the same as CHRIST JESUS ....
humbled even to accepting death, death on a cross.'

It never crossed JESUS' mind to say anything like that little child of a few pages before 'but you wouldn't want me to have lost, would you daddy?' On the contrary He who was LORD over all things let others 'lord it over him' that He might in turn free them from that which would destroy them. Recall His words to Pilate during His trial, *'You would have no power over me lest I gave it to you'.*

What a tremendous lesson for us!

How many times have we recoiled at another's authority over us?

108

- when we were children at home with our parents …
- when we were at school with our teachers …
- when at work with our bosses
    - or even -
- our work colleagues who might be in charge of our shift or the activity that we are presently engaged in
- in our Religious Community during times of formation …
- with our spouses when we have felt that 'we have not been listened to'

Take a few moments to think about the times in your life when you have resented people 'lording it over you' and see if in your heart you are still smoldering under the memory and still resent the incident.

If there are such times these will need to be addressed because they will affect our relationships with anyone who tries to point something out to us. We will be affected no matter how small the issue might be even if it is advice on how to use a cork screw or how to use a tube of toothpaste. If we do not deal with this issue then we will find ourselves growing in the area of resentment and that is not the way of someone who has been invited to *'live through love in His presence'*.

And o'er its own shortcomings weeps with loathing

St. Dominic, the founder of the Dominican Order, once gave this piece of advice to one of his early brethren: 'If you cannot weep for the world, learn to weep for your own sins'.

Let us take some time to put our sins under the microscope of GOD'S love for us. Let us examine our sins under the light of love shed from the cross. Let us see what our sins look like when compared to the love that GOD has for us, a love that redeemed us through the blood of His only begotten SON.

Let us dare to take an honest glimpse at our sins. We might even have the courage to pray: 'Lord, show me the effect that my sins have had on the life of others and on myself.' St. Paul speaks of 'those things that now make you blush', in the light of love itself do our sins make us blush? Are we led to the point where we think that if we were to look on them any longer we would 'die of shame'? Of course, this is not the point of the exercise. GOD does not want us to die in our shame but to recognise the new life that He has won for us and to ask for His mercy and forgiveness. No one can do this for us. This is something that we need to do for ourselves. That is why the habit of going regularly to the Sacrament of Reconciliation is so tremendous because it is during this Sacrament that we receive the absolution of our sins and the grace that we need to 'not sin again'.

The invitation that St. Paul throws out to the early Church in Rome is to be: *'Dead to sin and alive to CHRIST'*.

Let us take up the challenge and through the mercy and grace of GOD, seek to give up the one thing that is really important; and that is to give up sinning. [21]

Ponder these words of Psalm 31:
'Happy is the man whose offence is forgiven,
whose sin is remitted.
O happy the man to whom the LORD
imputes no guilt,
in whose spirit is no guile.

But now I have acknowledged my sins;
my guilt I did not hide.
I said: 'I will confess
my offence to the LORD.'
And you, LORD, have forgiven
the guilt of my sin.

Rejoice, rejoice in the LORD,
exult, you just!
O come, ring out your joy,
all you upright of heart.'

The Lord is truly great because He wants us to be at peace in all areas of our life and with all people who we are in relationship with. In order for this to become more and more a reality we need to continually seek the forgiveness and mercy of GOD. Through His Church we do have the means of receiving that forgiveness direct from Himself in the Sacrament of Reconciliation.

May I suggest that you take time to re-read this last verse and the reflections on each line and see if there is, at this moment, anything that you need to bring to this incredible sacrament then please receive the Sacrament as soon as you can.

We read in the Catechism of the Catholic Church, paragraph 1446: 'CHRIST instituted the sacrament of Penance for all sinful members of His Church: above all for those who, since Baptism, have fallen into grave sin, and have lost their baptismal grace and wounded ecclesial communion. It is to them that the sacrament of Penance offers a new possibility to convert and to recover the grace of justification. The Fathers of the Church present this sacrament as 'the second plank (of salvation) after the shipwreck which is the loss of grace.' Earlier we read in paragraph 1443: 'During His public life JESUS not only forgave sins, but also made plain the effect of this forgiveness: He re-integrated forgiven sinners in to the community of the People of GOD from which sin had alienated or even excluded them. A remarkable sign of this is the fact that JESUS receives sinners at His table, a gesture that expresses in an astonishing way both GOD'S forgiveness and the return to the bosom of the People of GOD.'

JESUS wants to bring healing and reconciliation into every area of your life. He asks you the same question as He asked in the gospels: *'What do you want me to do for you?'*[22]

This is the time to respond to that question for yourself; to search your life and see where you are in need of healing and reconciliation and run to meet Him on the road where He has already started to run towards you just as the father ran to the boy in the parable of the prodigal son.

If you know of anything in your life where there is a block to you being at one with the people of GOD do not hesitate, if you have the opportunity, to go to the Sacrament of Reconciliation. After admitting to those sins which separate you not only from GOD but also from other people rejoice as you hear these words spoken to you by the priest:

'GOD, the Father of mercies,
through the death and resurrection of His SON
has reconciled the world to Himself
and sent the HOLY SPIRIT among us
for the forgiveness of sins;
through the ministry of the Church
may GOD give you pardon and peace,
and I absolve you of all your sins
in the name of the FATHER, and of the SON,
and of the HOLY SPIRIT.'

Ponder these words of the formulae of Absolution and then make the time to receive the Sacrament of Reconciliation. It might be an idea to take one of your favourite passages in Sacred Scripture where JESUS is forgiving someone and read it over a period of a couple of days.

When you have finished your reflections of the passage make contact with a priest and ask if he could hear your confession. You might even like to explain that this is a part of a retreat that you are taking yourself through at home. This will give the priest the understanding that you have taken time over your confession and he will then ensure that your Sacrament of Reconciliation is not done in a hurried way. However, if you would just like to go anonymously during a regular time for Confessions in your Church that will be as blessed. GOD knows what has been going on in the secret of your heart and how you have prepared yourself in the quiet of your own home for this Sacrament.

Then all that remains is to try and respond to the graces that you receive in the Sacrament knowing with every confidence that 'by the help of your (GOD'S) grace you will not sin again'.

For those who are not Roman Catholic

You might like to take a moment at this stage and follow through the same steps above but when it comes to the administering of the Sacrament of Penance you might like to make the opportunity of speaking to a minister from your own Church, or going to someone who you know and trust who will pray with you about the things you would like GOD to forgive you for.

Prayer Ministry

At this point of your reflection you might like to think about receiving some form of Prayer Ministry, again from someone you trust. You might like to ask the person praying for you to pray a prayer of 'Healing of Memories' in order that your past will not continue to affect your future by bringing up 'negative triggers'.

A note about Prayer Ministry. Prayer Ministry involves the 'Laying on of Hands' [23] Usually two people, one of either sex, prays with you. They would lay their hands, with your permission, perhaps on your shoulder and head, maybe on your back and they would then simply ask GOD, to send the HOLY SPIRIT to come and heal you – physically, emotionally or spiritually. The prayer does not need to be a long prayer. Those praying may have the Gift of Tongues and would use this gift at this time as well as the Gift of Prophesy or Words of Knowledge. All of which are gifts of the HOLY SPIRIT and are an aid to the prayer that is taking place. I will deliberately not go into too much detail here for I would rather that you experienced this prayer with very little pre-conceived ideas of what might happen because then GOD is free, in the power of the HOLY SPIRIT, to move in your life. It is far better to have an open mind and heart in this prayer than to go expecting GOD to move in a certain way.

Moving forward into new life in Christ

The most important thing is to make a decision to live in co-operation with all the graces that GOD gives you and where possible to seek out those graces through; Personal Prayer; Liturgical Prayer - the Eucharist, The Divine Office; reading Sacred Scripture; reading the Fathers of the Church; attending the Sacraments of the Church; seeking the companionship and the activities that would enable you to grow in your life of faith rather than those which would detract from it.

To grow in faith means that we have to make certain personal choices. It is never automatic. GOD gives us the graces as free gift. We have to then learn to recognise those graces when they are given to us and then to do all that we can to create within ourselves an environment where those graces can take root and then be enabled to bear fruit.

Remember in the journey of faith GOD is always the prime mover. He always takes the initiative. It is for us to respond. In John's Gospel we read:
'You did not choose me,
no, I chose you;
and I commissioned you
to go out and to bear fruit,
fruit that will last.'   *(John 15:16)*

In verse 17 we have the core of the Gospel message: *'What I command you is to love one another.'*

This is such a challenge for He commands us to love but the measure of our love is the measure with which He has loved us and that is to die for us whilst we were still sinners. Can we, knowing this, refuse love or forgiveness to anyone? If our answer is 'yes' then we haven't really begun on the journey of life and GOD then issues us with an invitation *'Repent and believe the Good News'*. Let us then pray for the desire to love as He has loved us, acknowledging that the first step is probably to discover just how much GOD has loved us and continues to love us. For His words are not mere words but His words have quite literally become flesh.

> *'He was in the world*
> *that had its being through Him,*
> *and the world did not know Him.*
> *He came to His own domain*
> *.. And His own people did not accept Him.'* *(John 1: 10-11)*

Let us take the time to read through the Gospel narratives again and pray as we do so the words of Mary, our Mother, at the Annunciation account: *'Let what you have said be done to me.'*

As we read the texts of Sacred Scripture let us continually ask that the Word, through the power of the HOLY SPIRIT would become 'flesh' in us. St. Ambrose one of the Father's of the Church once wrote: *'Every soul that believes conceives and generates the word of GOD.'*

Let us become not just 'hearers' of the Word but if you like 'livers' of the Word. May the Word of GOD take root and grow in our lives that the prologue to St. John's

Gospel may truly be fulfilled one day in our lives:
'But to all who did accept Him
he gave power to become children of GOD,
to all who believe in the name of Him
who was born not out of human stock
or the urge of flesh
or the will of man
but of GOD Himself.' *(John 1:11-13)*

- Let us become Christians.
- Let us become 'Christ-bearers'.
- Let us bear fruit - fruit that will last.
- Let us become children of GOD fulfilling His command to love others as He has loved us.
- Let holy charity our outward vesture be and lowliness our inner clothing

May we have true lowliness of heart
which always seeks the humbler part
and o'er our own shortcomings
may we weep with loathing.
AMEN

Notes to Verse Three

17. We soon find out that if we operate only in the power of our own will that we soon fall short of the goal that we want to achieve. In other words, our own will power is never enough to overcome the things and situations that we find hard.

18. One of my confessions in my late teens was about my inability to forgive someone who had hurt me and my family greatly. I received a great deal of comfort when the priest, who later became, and remains, my Spiritual Director, said to me the great words of encouragement, 'Maria, you might forgive the person today or tomorrow. It might take you five years, ten years, twenty years. Indeed, you might never be able to forgive them before you die but what GOD wants is that you want to forgive them not that you have forgiven them.' This was a major step in being able to live with unforgiveness which later turned in to forgiveness after many years.

19. Another form of praying with the cross is to take it gently in your hands and then simply slowly kiss the five wounds of JESUS: His feet, His hands, His side, His head. Then say: AMEN.

20. You might like to use this as a Lenten Meditation or as a means of preparing for the Sacrament of Reconciliation or for a prayer for the Healing of Memories.

21. A few years ago just before Lent was to begin I prayed and asked GOD what HE wanted me to give up for Lent. As a member of a Religious Community who didn't normally watch television I usually gave up chocolate and puddings and couldn't see that there was much else to give up. Then one day in my prayer I felt GOD say, 'Why don't you give up sinning for Lent?' This I tried to do and have never been so conscious of how many times I sin each day than during that Lent. I would like to say that I kept the 'fast' going long afterwards but I am sorry to say that I didn't, though in truth, with the grace of GOD I would like to be able to.

22. Luke 18: 21

23. The 'Laying on of Hands' for healing stems from the times that JESUS HIMSELF healed people through touch, i.e. cure of the Leper, Matthew 8: 1-4; Mark 1: 40-45; Luke 5: 12-16; cure of Peter's Mother-in-Law, Matthew 8: 14-5; Mark 1: 29-31; Cure of the two blind men, Matthew 9: 27-31; Jairus' daughter raised to life, Mark 5: 35-43, Luke 8: 49-56; Blind man at Bethsaida, Mark 8: 22-26.

Verse Four

And so the yearning strong,
with which my soul will long,
shall far outpass the power of human telling;
for none can guess its grace,
till he become the place
wherein the HOLY SPIRIT makes its dwelling.

And so the yearning strong

How would you sum up your relationship with GOD at this moment? Having heard Him ask you personally 'What do you want me to do for you?' Have you taken the opportunity yet to let go of all that you

121

knew of GOD up until now to be filled with the peace and mercy that the disciples experienced for themselves after the resurrection?

Is GOD, the GOD of your making, matching up to your image and likeness or have you dared to allow Him to be what He truly is for all of us: the omnipotent GOD, FATHER, SON and HOLY SPIRIT. The GOD who, out of HIS infinite love, made us in His image and likeness. The GOD who became man, flesh of our flesh, coming into the world that had its being through Him that He might die and suffer not to be just the GOD of all creation but to be the GOD who wrought our salvation, the GOD of our redemption.

Are you, as the psalmist writes, yearning for GOD in the same way that a deer thirsts for running water. GOD, indeed, is thirsting for you. The question remains, though, 'How thirsty are you for Him?'

The catechism of the Catholic Church writes in paragraph 2560: 'If only you knew the gift of GOD!' The wonder of prayer is revealed there beside the well where we come seeking water: there, CHRIST comes to meet every human being. It is He who first seeks us and asks us for a drink. JESUS thirsts; His asking arises from the depths of GOD'S desire for us. Whether we realise it or not, prayer is the encounter of GOD'S thirst with ours. GOD thirsts that we might thirst for Him.'

I repeat, 'How thirsty are you for GOD?'

Our thirst for GOD parallels our knowledge of Him. For the more we go to the source of our **salvation** the more we will discover that there is so much more to GOD than we can ever even comprehended or imagined.

He is **The Fountain of Living Water** that will never dry up no matter how much we drink from its life giving waters. No matter how many times we come drinking love from this source of love, or how many billions of others throughout the different generations come seeking these waters it will never be diminished. It will not decrease even one drop because it is truly the source of life itself and thus is infinite for infinity.

How eager are you for the things of GOD?

We read in John 20:2-6: *'They have taken the LORD out of the tomb' she said 'and we don't know where they've put Him.' So Peter set out with the other disciple to go to the tomb. They* **ran** *together, but the other disciple, running faster, reached the tomb first; ...'*

How eager are you for the things of GOD?

Are you prepared to quite literally run in order that you might even glimpse Him as He passes.

On the mornings when you prepare to go to Church does your heart beat with eager longing until you arrive at your FATHER'S house?

Does your heart-rate increase and burn within you as you turn the last familiar corner knowing you are but a few feet away from the very presence of GOD Himself.

Does your heart rise up in greeting within you as the Eucharistic Species, CHRIST present in the Blessed Sacrament, is raised high above all heads so that all may glimpse their LORD and Maker?

Does your heart quicken as the Precious Blood of the spotless Lamb is lifted in the Cup of Redemption?

OR ..... are we caught up in a fight going on within ourselves wanting to be wholly present and yet distracted by so many ordinary thoughts.

Is there even a fight going on within, that one could be elsewhere if we didn't have this 'duty' to fulfil?

Are we annoyed because this 'precious time' is eating away at our 'free time' when instead of being here, we could be doing a hundred and one other important things?

Is our mind so caught up with the myriad of things of life that we have not really noticed any actions since we awoke in the morning till when we put our hand on the handle of the Church door?

Is this just another thing that we are trying to squeeze into an already over-busy life?

How eager are you for the things of GOD? How eager are you for GOD Himself?

*'When they drew near to the village to which they were going, He made as if to go on; but they **pressed Him** to stay with them.' (Luke 24: 28)*
When our time of prayer is drawing to a close do we rush to finish it? or do we earnestly long for GOD to turn the clock back that we might have our time with Him again and if possible to stop the clock that we might have an infinite moment with Him? Do we indeed want Him to stop time altogether that we might have just a taste of what is to come in eternity being caught up in the Triune GODHEAD even here and now?

How earnest are we?

Are we like the bride in the Song of Songs who loudly professes her love for her intended spouse but when he comes in the early morning and knocks at her door she gets annoyed at the untimely inconvenience of the visit.

He knocks but she complains. He knocks but she is slow
to respond to love and this being the case finds her
beloved gone when at last she finally opens the door to
him:

'I sleep but my heart is awake.
I hear my beloved knocking.
'Open to me, my sister, my love,
my dove, my perfect one,
for my head is covered with dew,
my locks with the drops of the night.'
'I have taken off my tunic,
am I to put it on again?
I have washed my feet,
Am I to dirty them again."
My beloved thrust his hand
Through the hole in the door;
I trembled to the core of my being.
Then I arose
To open to my Beloved,
myrrh ran off my hands,
pure myrrh off my fingers,
on to the handle of the bolt.
I opened to my Beloved,
but he had turned his back and gone!
My soul failed at his flight.
I sought him but I could not find him,
I called to him but he did not answer.' (Song of Songs 5: 2-6)

Was she really in love or was it mere words? Was it just words until he had gone and then she realised that she was actually in love? The two disciples on the road to Emmaus didn't know that JESUS was actually with them until after He had vanished from their sight and then they exclaimed: *'Did not our heats burn within us as He talked to us along the road and explained the scriptures to us?'* *(Luke 24: 32)*

The women who came to anoint the body of JESUS had a similar experience: *'They found that the stone had been rolled away from the tomb, but on entering discovered that the body of JESUS was not there. As they stood there not knowing what to think, two men in brilliant clothes appeared at their side. Terrified, the women lowered their eyes. But the two men said to them, "Why look among the dead for someone who is alive? He is not here; He has **risen.'*** *(Luke 24:2-5)*

If only they had kept vigil at His tomb they might not have lost Him. How much of our faith journey is built on 'If only'?

- If only I had gone with you then I would have had the same experience as you have had.
- If only I had not fallen asleep during the sermon this week then I would have not missed the same uplifting words that you have heard.

There again if we don't live out our faith on the 'If only' we might be those who live out our faith from past experiences, never opening ourselves up to what GOD might be wanting to do for us in this present moment.

Even worse, we might live out our faith journey purely on other people's experiences. Do you recall Chapter 3 of Exodus when YAHWEH revealed who He was to Moses by saying: *'My name is I AM, I AM who AM.* JESUS Himself told the scribes and the Pharisees: *'Before ever Abraham was, I AM.'* This is not the GOD of the past or the future but quite clearly, GOD is GOD of the present. HE is also the GOD of all that had life through Him recalling the opening words of John's Gospel: *'Through Him all things came to be, not one thing had its being but through Him. All that came to be had life in Him.'* *(John 1: 2-3)*

He is the GOD of the entire creation and at the same time a personal GOD to those who individually came to have life through Him. GOD is very much a personal GOD who comes and knocks on the door of each person's soul asking each one individually if He might make His home in them. He knocks continually on the door of each of our souls but let us take heed from the words of the Song of Songs and not delay too long in answering to Him lest He move on and like the women at the tomb, we can no longer find Him. Let us be instead like Peter and John who ran in the direction of where they knew the LORD might be coming. Let us not wait for Him to knock but let us rise before the early morning dew and rush out to meet Him as He rises to greet us with the gift of the new life of the Resurrection. Let us build on the faith of yesterdays by opening ourselves to what GOD would do for us or have us do for Him, **today**.

So, the invitation is clear and St. Paul wastes no time in issuing it to the people of Ephesus: *'Wake up from your sleep, rise from the dead, and CHRIST will enlighten you.'* *(Ephesians 5: 14)*

But the question remains: 'Do you really care?' Are you thirsting for Him as much as He thirsts for you? Is your desire to receive the fulness of life in Him as great as His desire is for you to have it? The answer on our part might be 'not really' but on GOD'S part there is no hint of the diminishing of His thirst for us. He has died in our stead that we might gain His life and so live as He would have us live – live life to the full.

With which the soul will long

St. Leo the Great once wrote: 'Christian, recognise your dignity and, now that you share in GOD'S own nature, do not return to your former base selves. Remember who is your head and whose body you now are. Never forget that you have been rescued from the powers of darkness and brought into the light of the Kingdom of GOD.' (Catechism 1619)

Adam and Eve were created naked but neither, we are told by the Genesis writer, felt any shame.[24] The reason for this is that they had both been created in a perfect state of being. When Adam, meaning first man, turned from God and committed the first sin which was to affect all creation as 'Original Sin', Adam and Eve knew shame for the first time and sought to hide their bodies from each other and also to hide their shame from GOD. When GOD subsequently finds them He covers their shame by making clothes for each of them out of animal skin. This clothing was temporary and indeed temporal. When JESUS, the second Adam, the SON of GOD and SON of Man died on the cross He did so naked. In doing so He restored to man his former dignity but He went further because when He rose from the dead JESUS clothed man not just in restored dignity and justification but also in JESUS' own righteousness.

St. Paul in his letter to the Ephesians refers to us as: *'GOD'S work of art, created in CHRIST JESUS to live the good life as from the beginning HE had intended us to live it.' (Ephesians 2: 10)*

This begs the questions of us:

- Do we accept that we are GOD'S work of art?
- Do we believe that we are priceless because we have been bought into righteousness by the blood of CHRIST Himself?

St. Thomas Aquinas, the famous Dominican theologian would tell us that in order to redeem mankind it only needed JESUS to shed just one drop of His blood, but He loved us completely and so He gave Himself completely. He gave us all that He could give us; He shed all His blood and entered into death, to triumph over death and bring with Him all whom He had redeemed through the shedding of His blood.

Catechism 1692 states: 'The symbol of the faith confesses the greatness of GOD'S gifts to man in His work of creation, and even more in redemption and sanctification. What faith confesses, the Sacraments communicate: by the Sacraments of rebirth, Christians have become children of GOD', partakers of the divine nature. Coming to see in the faith their new dignity, Christians are called henceforth to a life 'worthy of the gospel of CHRIST. They are made capable of doing so by the grace of CHRIST and the gifts of His SPIRIT, which they receive through the Sacraments and through prayer'.

Through our Baptism we became partakers in the divine

nature not, as St. Paul writes, because of anything we ourselves have done, no it is all GOD'S gift. Recall the words of St. Augustine to the newly baptised of his day: *'Rejoice! Rejoice! For you have become CHRIST'*.

We will never experience this new gift of life that we have been given, if we never open ourselves to a life of faith and respond to the graces that we have been given. The more we become 'Beggars before GOD' (St. Augustine) the more we shall experience in our lives the 'utter fulness of GOD' that St. Paul so confidently prays for the people of Ephesus to experience. If I am too proud to become a 'Beggar', God will always seem to be so far away and totally disinterested in anything to do with my life or of the lives of those around me. The more that I choose not to be a 'Beggar' the closer I will come to stating categorically that 'there is indeed no GOD anyway'. I will state very clearly so that everyone can hear me that there is no GOD and those around me who too refuse to become 'Beggars' take heed of my cry with welcome ears and even begin to cry with the same disdainful tone as I do. What pride! What insolence! Indeed, what utter stupidity! Man ultimately fooling himself that man indeed was clever enough to create man! How easy it is for man to place himself higher than GOD; but ponder for a second the stupidity of that statement for if there is no GOD, as many proclaim, to what heights can man rise, for if there is no GOD there are no heights to attain to!

As 'disciples of CHRIST', we are always invited to live in the light of the FATHER: *'Be like children of the light'* St. Paul exhorts us. In order to do this we need to heed the advice that YAHWEH gave to Moses and Aaron during the Exodus in the desert, *'Never leave the entrance to the Tent of Meeting.'* Never, therefore, leave the place of the Covenant, never leave 'the will of GOD' by turning our will to His.

I have already spoken about having the same mind as CHRIST and if we choose of our will to become 'Beggars before GOD' we will always and in all things only seek to discover the will of GOD and then to carry it out in all things. I will freely choose to die to self so that the will of GOD can be carried out in my life and in the lives of those around me. Hebrews 9: 15-17 speaks of the power of the new covenant brought about by the death of JESUS, the fulfillment of the FATHER'S will: *'He brings a new covenant, as the mediator, only so that the people who were called to an eternal inheritance may actually receive what is promised: His death took place to cancel the sins that infringed the earlier covenant. Now, wherever a will is in question, the death of the testator must be established; indeed, it only becomes valid with that death, since it is not meant to have any effect whilst the testator is still alive.'*

CHRIST fulfilled the new covenant with His death. Is it too much to ask that we would align our wills with the one who died to make us co-heirs with Himself, raising us to a state for all eternity which would be higher than the angels? How little the cost to us to become 'Beggars before God', to 'die to self' that we might 'put on the mind of CHRIST' and know without any shadow of doubt 'what hope His call has for us'.

Of JESUS it is said:
'... and this is what He said on coming into the world:
You who wanted no sacrifice or oblation
prepared a body for me.
You who took no pleasure in holocausts
or sacrifices for sin;
then I said,
just as I was commanded in the scroll of the book,
'GOD, here I am!
I am coming to obey your will.' (Hebrews 10: 5-6)

What can we cry but an echo with the psalmist who wrote: *'What nation has a GOD so great as ours!'*

We read in Hebrews 10:14: *'By virtue of that one single offering, He has achieved the eternal perfection of all whom He is sanctifying.'*

The writer of Hebrews continues in verses 14-17:
'The HOLY SPIRIT assures us of this; for He says; first:
This is the covenant I will make with them when those

days arrive;
and the LORD goes on to say:
I will put my laws into their hearts
And write them on their minds.
I will never call their sins to mind
or their offences.'

Let our souls long only for the things of GOD, let us take pleasure in nothing but delighting in the LORD our GOD. Let us train ourselves that our souls will only be at home in the things of GOD. May we strive to 'live through love in His presence' with our souls resting in Him who thirsts for us to have life and live it to the full.

'As the doe longs
for running streams,
so longs my soul
for you, my GOD.

My soul thirsts for GOD,
the GOD of my life;
when shall I go to see
the face of GOD?

I have no food but tears,
day and night;
and all day long men say to me,
'Where is your GOD?'

I remember, and my soul
melts within me:
I am on my way to the wonderful Tent,
to the house of GOD,
among cries of joy and praise
and an exultant throng.

Why so downcast, my soul
why do you sigh within me?
Put your hope in GOD: I shall praise Him yet,
my saviour, my GOD.' (Psalm 42)

Shall far outpass the power of human telling

There is still so much more! We read in the Catechism,
paragraph 460: 'The Word became flesh to make us partakers
of the divine nature'. (2 Peter 1:4) 'For this is why the Word
became man, and the SON of GOD became Son of man; so that
man, by entering into communion with the Word and thus
receiving divine sonship, might become a Son of GOD.'
(St. Irenaus) 'The only-begotten SON of GOD, wanting to make
us sharers in His DIVINITY, assumed our nature, so that He,
made man, might make men gods'. (St. Thomas Aquinas, O.P.)

GOD has given us quite literally everything because He loves us. He has even given us a share in His own nature. Something that our first parents did not participate in but because of their fall from grace we in some way rejoice because it is because they sinned that GOD became man and took on our fallen human nature: in order to raise us up with Himself. The Exultet, the great song of praise which is sung by the priest at the Easter Vigil exclaims so profoundly 'O happy fault, O necessary sin of Adam.'

Once we were but thoughts in the mind of GOD but to what heights He has died to raise us to, for JESUS says Himself *'When I am lifted up I shall draw all men to myself.'*

We who fell from grace, have been lifted to a state higher than before the fall. And yet, in spite of all we know of GOD'S tremendous love for us we freely choose to go on sinning against Him! We turn our gaze from the light because we find it more 'comfortable' to live in the dark. JESUS asked the blind man, *'What do you want?'* He replied, *'That I might see!'* Our own lives would be so different if only we too would humble ourselves to cry out, *'Son of David have pity on me!'* How our lives would change if we went to the sacrament of Penance truly contrite, but isn't it the truth that we are more afraid of experiencing the weight of our own sin than we are of wanting to rejoice in the mercy of GOD? Sadly, the reality is also that sometimes we don't even care about the effect of our sin on ourselves and those around us. Participating in the Sacrament of Penance is the last thing on our minds.

In John Chapter 4 we read these simple words that JESUS says to the Samaritan woman, *'If only you knew the gift of GOD.'* If only we would know the gift of GOD we would not want to commit another transgression against His steadfastness and love towards us, let alone the long list that we so half-heartedly repeat to ourselves, priests and others.

Let us not plead so earnestly for the gifts of the HOLY SPIRIT, the gifts of tongues and prophesy, for example, let us with bended knee plead for the gifts of humility and love, for the grace to resist temptation at all times. Let us earnestly work for the salvation of our own souls and the desire for the salvation of everyone else past, present and future.

For none can guess its grace

Mary, the lowly handmaid of the LORD said her fiat to GOD when she said to the angel Gabriel, *'Let what you have said be done.'* Then she conceived Him who had given her life and conceived her immaculate so that the angel rightly greeted her by saying, *'Hail Mary, full of grace.'*

Through the gift of GOD Mary was conceived 'full of grace'. Like her son she would grow in 'wisdom and understanding' of the gift that had been given her and the call that it had placed on her life from its beginning.

GOD had chosen her from among all women throughout the course of time to be the Mother of His only-begotten SON.

We are told that, *'When a man has had a great deal given him on trust, even more will be expected of him'.   (Luke 12: 48)* Mary had been given a great gift but the cost, in choosing to assent with her will to the will of GOD, would be great. As Simeon prophesied when JESUS was presented in the Temple. *'Now in Jerusalem there was a man named Simeon. He was an upright and devout man; he looked forward to Israel's comforting and the HOLY SPIRIT rested on him. It had been revealed to him by the HOLY SPIRIT that he would not see death until he had set his eyes on the CHRIST of the LORD. Prompted by the SPIRIT he came to the Temple: and when the parents brought in the child JESUS to do for HIM what the Law required, he took him into his arms and blessed GOD; and he said: 'Now, Master, you can let your servant go in peace, just as you promised; because my eyes have seen the salvation which you have prepared for all the nations to see, a light to enlighten the pagans and the glory of your people Israel.'   As the child's father and mother stood there wondering at the things that were being said about Him, Simeon blessed them and said to His mother, 'You see this child: He is destined for the fall and for the rising of many in Israel, destined to be a sign that is rejected – and a sword will pierce your own soul too – so that the secret thoughts of many may be laid bare.' (Luke 2: 25-35)*

If we look up grace in the index of the Catholic Catechism we can see quite clearly some of the things that we might need to know about grace. Grace is a gift from GOD, bestowed on us through the HOLY SPIRIT: 'Grace is first and foremost the gift of the SPIRIT who justifies us and sanctifies us. But grace also includes the gifts that the SPIRIT grants us to associate us with HIS work, to enable us to collaborate in the salvation of others and in the growth of the BODY of CHRIST. There are sacramental graces, gifts proper to the different sacraments. There are furthermore special graces, also called charisms after the Greek term used by St. Paul and meaning 'favour', 'gratuitous gift', 'benefit'. Whatever their character – sometimes it is extraordinary, such as the gift of miracles or of tongues – charisms are orientated towards sanctifying grace, and are intended for the common good of the CHURCH. They are at the service of charity which builds up the Church.' (Catechism, Paragraph 2003)

Paragraph 2011 explains further: 'The charity of CHRIST is the source in us of all our merits before GOD. Grace, by uniting us to CHRIST in active love, ensures the supernatural quality of our acts and consequently their merit before GOD and before men. The saints have always had a lively awareness that their merits were pure grace: 'After earth's exile, I hope to go and enjoy you in the fatherland, but I do not want to lay up merits for heaven. I want to work for your love alone ... In the evening of this life, I shall appear before you with empty hands, for I do not ask you, LORD, to count on my works. All our justice is blemished in your eyes. I wish, then, to be clothed in your own justice and to receive from your love the eternal possession of yourself.' (St. Therese of Lisieux, 'Act of Offering' in Story of a Soul)

Need we search any more? To understand that grace 'unites us to CHRIST in active love' so clearly tells us of our need for grace and that without it all that we would do or say is only for ourselves. Let us 'run and not grow weary' in the path of grace. Let us place ourselves ever ready at the source of grace that we would be 'associated with the work of the HOLY SPIRIT' enabling us to 'collaborate in the salvation of others and in the building up of the Body of CHRIST'. Can we find any purpose in life greater than this? Is there anything that we can do of ourselves that can measure up to this? Plainly the answer is 'No!'

Let us waste no more time, let us take our cue from Mary, our Mother and cry out our fiat to GOD once and for all, let us pray in earnest, *'Let what you have said be done to me'.*

GOD had invited the first man to: *'Be fruitful, multiply, fill the earth and conquer it. Be masters of the fish of the sea, the birds of heaven and all living animals on the earth.' (Gen. 1:28)* JESUS said to His first disciples: *'All authority in heaven and on earth has been given to me. Go, therefore, make disciples of all the nations; baptise them in the name of the FATHER and of the SON and of the HOLY SPIRIT, and teach them to observe all the commands I gave you.' (Matthew 28:19-20)*

In the Acts of the Apostles, also written by Luke we read: *'It is not for you to know times or dates that the FATHER has decided by His own authority, but you will receive power when the HOLY SPIRIT comes on you, and then you will be my witness ...' (Acts 1: 7-8)*

He has called us all to *'Go out and bear fruit, fruit that will last'*. St. Paul tells us that the only thing that will last is LOVE. Let our love not be illusory but real. Let our love be that which we receive through grace and comes flowing from the wound in the side of CHRIST. Let us love as He has loved us. Let us love with the same love with which He has loved us. Let us shine with His light and become lights in our own world 'not hidden under a tub but exposed on the hill-top' so that all peoples can not only see but be challenged to move up out of their darkness and become lights themselves.

It is a tremendous calling and we will never reach the

depths of the grace that GOD wants to bestow on us that His kingdom might come 'on earth as it is in heaven'.

St. Paul puts is so plainly: *'You were darkness once, but now you are light in the LORD; be like children of the light, for the effects of the light are seen in complete goodness and right living and truth. Try to discover what the LORD wants of you, having nothing to do with the futile works of darkness but exposing them by contrast. The things that are done in secret are things that people are even ashamed to think of; but anything exposed by the light will be illuminated and anything illuminated turns into light'* (Ephesians 5:8-14)

Take the time to reflect on the words of this hymn and then turn the words into a prayer:

Come, HOLY SPIRIT, live in us
With GOD the FATHER and the SON,
And grant us your abundant grace
To sanctify and make us one.

May mind and tongue made strong in love,
Your praise throughout the world proclaim,
And may that love within our hearts
Set fire to others with its flame.

Most blessed TRINITY of love
For whom the heart of man was made
To you be praise in timeless song
And everlasting homage made.   Amen

Till he become the place

And JESUS prayed:
  'I pray not only for these,
  but for those also
  who through their words will believe in me.
  May they all be one.
  FATHER, may they be one in us,
  as you are in me and I am in you,
  so that the world may believe
  that it was you who sent me.
  I have given them the glory you gave to me,
  that they may be one as we are one.
  With me in them and you in me,
  may they be so completely one
  that the world will realise that it was you who sent me
  and that I have loved them
  as much as you have loved me.

144

FATHER,
I want those you have given me
to be with me where I am,
so that they may always see the glory
you have given me
because you loved me before the foundation of the
world.' (John 17:20-24)

JESUS prayed this prayer for us, for you and me. The night before He died He prayed that we would 'be with me where I am'. If we do not understand by now how much we have been loved and will be loved for all eternity one wonders if there will ever be anything that will convince us. JESUS has died to take away the barrier that separated us from Him and has prayed for us that we would be with Him for all eternity.

Let us become simple and say the only thing that can be said to such a tremendous offer from GOD for us, and that is to say: AMEN!

In the movement of life, GOD, as has already been said, is the 'prime mover'. He initiates all life but it is for us, the 'crown of His creation' to receive the gift of life, to work with it, and to grow in it.

GOD is the initiator of the gift but He goes further in

giving us the gift of His grace that enables us to live life as fully as He intended us to live it.

The gift is His but the response is ours. If it were not, GOD would indeed be the greatest puppeteer that ever was and we would all be fools to believe that He was anything other.

To prove that He is not a puppeteer and that we are not His puppets all we have to do is ponder our sins. Sins are proof positive of GOD'S incredible gift to us of Free Will, for the very act of sinning means that we choose a way other than GOD'S way for us. We choose to act independently from GOD and no puppet, no matter how sophisticated, can act other than always at the will of the one who 'holds the strings'.

To see once again how much GOD loves us we only need to read the following words of St. Basil (Catechism, paragraph 736): 'Through the HOLY SPIRIT we are restored to paradise, led back to the kingdom of heaven and adopted as children, given confidence to call GOD 'FATHER' and to share in CHRIST'S grace, called children of light and given a share in eternal glory.'

Let us respond again, AMEN! So be it, I agree with what has been done for me.

Wherein the Holy Spirit makes His dwelling[25]

So, now what do we ask of GOD?
What do you ask of GOD?
Do you now cry with all your heart, mind and soul:

'Come down, O love divine
seek thou this soul of mine
and visit it with thine own ardour glowing.' ?

If we dare to use this song as a prayer we will feel a song welling up within our hearts, a deep burning in our soul that compels us once more to join with Mary and cry, once again: *'Let what you have said be done to me.'*

The HOLY SPIRIT is hovering over us, as He hovered over the void before time began. He is hovering and waiting for us to cry for ourselves:

- 'Let there be light in my life.'
- 'Let there now be order in the chaos.'
- 'Let me be aware of the effect that sin has on my life and on the lives of those around me.'
- 'Let me be 'holy and spotless and live in love in His presence'.[26]

- 'Let me 'become His adopted child, for His own kind purposes, to praise the glory of His grace, His free gift to me in the **Beloved**.' [27]
- 'Let me be 'dead to sin and alive to CHRIST.' [28]
- 'Let me offer my life as a holy sacrifice, truly pleasing to GOD. Not modelled on the world around me, but with my behaviour changed, modelled by my new mind.' [29]
- 'Let me no longer live an aimless life.' [30]
- 'Let me live a life worthy of my vocation.' [31]
- 'Let me be the child of GOD that He intended me to be from the very beginning. The child that has a role in His plan for creation.

St. Paul writes: *'This may be a wicked age, but your lives should redeem it.'* [32]

Let me, let us, play our part in the History of Salvation. Let us allow ourselves to be overshadowed by the HOLY SPIRIT and become a dwelling place for the divine.

Let us conclude by joining with Mary, our Mother and the Mother of GOD, in her Magnificat:

Tell out my soul,
the greatness of the LORD!
Unnumbered blessings, give my spirit voice;
Tender to me the promise of his word;
In GOD my Saviour shall my soul rejoice.

Tell out, my soul,
the greatness of His name!
Make known His might, the deeds His arm has done;
His mercy sure, from age to age the same;
His holy name, the Lord, the mighty one.

Tell out, my soul,
the greatness of His might!
Powers and dominions lay their glories by.
Proud hearts and stubborn wills are put to flight,
The hungry fed, the humble lifted high.

Tell out, my soul,
the glories of His word!
Firm is His promise, and His mercy sure.
Tell out my soul, the greatness of the Lord
To children's children and for evermore!

AMEN.

Notes to Verse Four:
24. Genesis 2:25
25. In the Sacrament of Baptism we become Temples of the Holy Spirit and this gift is confirmed in us in the Sacrament of Confirmation. In the Sacrament of Baptism the priest will say, 'Be baptised in the name of the FATHER, and of the SON and of the HOLY SPIRIT.' No 'Amen' is said in response. The prayer is completed in the Sacrament of Confirmation after the Bishop, or his delegate, says to the person being confirmed, 'Be sealed with the gift of the HOLY SPIRIT', to which the person responds, 'Amen'.
26. Ephesians 1:4
27. Ephesians 1: 4-6
28. Romans 6: 11
29: Romans 12: 1-2
30. Ephesians 4: 17
31. Ephesians 4: 1
32. Ephesians 5: 16

BIBLIOGRAPHY

The Jerusalem Bible: Students Edition:
Publishers: Darton, Longman and Todd.

Catechism of the Catholic Church:
Publishers: Geoffrey Chapman

Dictionary of Biblical Theology: Xavier Leon-DuFour:
Publishers: Geoffrey Chapman.

The New Jerome Commentary; Edited by Raymond E.
Brown, Joseph A. Fitzmyer and Roland E. Murphy:
Publishers: Geoffrey Chapman

Renewal In The Spirit Of St. Dominic, William A.
Hinnebush, O.P. ; Copyright 1968 Dominicana. Printed in
America.

A Memorial Of A Christian Life, F. Lewis De Granda, O.P.;
Revised and Corrected By F. J. L'Estrange, O.C.D.; Ninth
Edition. 1881. Publishers: James Duffy & Sons, 15
Wellington Quay and 1a Paternoster Row, London.

Further copies of this book
can be purchased from

Goodnews Books & Audio
15 Barking Close, Luton,
Beds. LU4 9HG
Tel: 01582 571011
fax: 01582 571012

order Christian books & music
by
phone, mail, or secure internet site:
www.goodnewsbooks.net
orders@goodnewsbooks.net